Table of Contents

Title Page

Copyright

Front Matter

Table of Contents

Introduction

Getting Started with ASP.NET Core

Setting Up Your Development Environment

Exploring the .NET Ecosystem

Understanding ASP.NET Core Architecture

Middleware Components

Dependency Injection in ASP.NET Core

Building Your First ASP.NET Core Application

Creating a Basic Web App

Running and Debugging Your Application

Routing and URL Management

Configuring Routes in ASP.NET Core

Advanced Routing Techniques

Working with Razor Pages

Creating Razor Pages

Using Razor Syntax for Dynamic Content

Controllers and Views

Implementing MVC Pattern

Managing Views and ViewModels

Data Access with Entity Framework Core

Setting Up Your Database Context

CRUD Operations with EF Core

Authentication and Authorization

Implementing Authentication Strategies

Role-Based Access Control in ASP.NET Core

Frontend Integration

Using JavaScript and CSS in ASP.NET Core

Single-Page Application Integration

Testing and Debugging ASP.NET Core
Applications

Writing Unit Tests

Using Debugging Tools Effectively

Deploying ASP.NET Core Applications

Preparing for Deployment

Cloud Deployment Options

Performance Optimization and Scalability

Caching Strategies for ASP.NET Core

Load Balancing and Scaling Techniques

Conclusion

Tools and Resources for ASP.NET Core
Development

ASP.NET Core Unlocked

Mastering Scalable Web Development

by

Callum V. Eversham

Although the author and publisher have made every effort to ensure that the information in this book was correct at press time, the author and publisher do not assume and hereby disclaim any liability to any party for any loss, damage, or disruption caused by errors or omissions, whether such errors or omissions result from negligence, accident, or any other cause.

This publication is designed to provide accurate and authoritative information with regard to the subject matter covered. It is sold with the understanding that the publisher is not engaged in rendering professional services. If legal advice or other expert assistance is required, the services of a competent professional should be sought.

The fact that an organization or website is referred to in this work as a citation and/or a potential source of further information does not mean that the author or the publisher endorses the information the organization or website may provide or recommendations it may make.

Please remember that Internet websites listed in this work may have changed or disappeared between when this work was written and when it is read.

ASP.NET Core Unlocked: Mastering Scalable Web Development

Contents

Introduction

Chapter 1: Getting Started with ASP.NET Core

Setting Up Your Development Environment

Exploring the .NET Ecosystem

Chapter 2: Understanding ASP.NET Core Architecture

Middleware Components

Dependency Injection in ASP.NET Core

Chapter 3: Building Your First ASP.NET Core Application

Creating a Basic Web App

Running and Debugging Your Application

Chapter 4: Routing and URL Management

Configuring Routes in ASP.NET Core

Advanced Routing Techniques

Chapter 5: Working with Razor Pages

Creating Razor Pages

Using Razor Syntax for Dynamic Content

Chapter 6: Controllers and Views

Implementing MVC Pattern

@Model.ProductName

Chapter 7: Data Access with Entity Framework Core

Setting Up Your Database Context

CRUD Operations with EF Core

Chapter 8: Authentication and Authorization

Implementing Authentication Strategies

Role-Based Access Control in ASP.NET Core

Chapter 9: Frontend Integration

Using JavaScript and CSS in ASP.NET Core

Single-Page Application Integration

Chapter 10: Testing and Debugging ASP.NET Core Applications

Writing Unit Tests

Using Debugging Tools Effectively

Chapter 11: Deploying ASP.NET Core Applications

Preparing for Deployment

Cloud Deployment Options

Chapter 12: Performance Optimization and Scalability

Caching Strategies for ASP.NET Core

Load Balancing and Scaling Techniques

Conclusion

Appendix A: Tools and Resources for ASP.NET Core Development

Introduction

In the ever-evolving world of web development, mastering a versatile and robust framework like ASP.NET Core is a vital skill for developers, both new and seasoned. As technology advances, the demand for highly performant, secure, and scalable applications continues to rise. ASP.NET Core stands out as a key player in meeting this demand, built on a foundation that offers developers the flexibility to create applications across multiple platforms without sacrificing quality or speed.

Why ASP.NET Core, you might ask? The answer lies in its ability to provide a modern, open-source, and cross-platform framework designed to meet the challenges of contemporary applications. It's engineered with performance in mind, providing lightning-fast processing capabilities that are essential for today's applications. Moreover, ASP.NET Core integrates seamlessly with front-end technologies, supporting developers in building rich client-side experiences while leveraging the extensive .NET ecosystem.

Our journey through this book is more than just an exploration of technical features and API functions; it's about cultivating a mindset that emphasizes best practices, efficiency, and innovation. We aim to empower you with the knowledge and skills to build scalable, maintainable applications that stand the test of time. As you delve into the intricate layers of ASP.NET Core, you'll encounter tools and methodologies that encourage clean, organized, and reusable code, reminiscent of software craftsmanship principles.

Navigating through the chapters, you will find a deliberate progression from setting up your development environment to advanced concepts like performance optimization and cloud deployment. This structure is designed to build a solid foundation while gradually introducing more complex topics. By the end, you'll not only be equipped with comprehensive technical knowledge but will also cultivate an adaptive mindset crucial for tackling the ever-changing landscape of software development.

One of the powerful aspects of ASP.NET Core is its architecture, which embraces the principles of modularity and configurability. By understanding and employing middleware components and leveraging dependency injection, you set the groundwork for clean, scalable applications. These architectural concepts are not merely technical constructs but are integral to developing solutions that are both robust and adaptable to change.

Building your first ASP.NET Core application may initially seem daunting, but fear not. With clear guidance and step-by-step instructions, this book will unravel complexities, and turn abstract concepts into tangible skills. From routing and URL management to the elegance of Razor Pages, each technique will be demystified, equipping you with practical understanding and hands-on experience.

Data management is another critical area where ASP.NET Core excels, thanks to its seamless integration with Entity Framework Core. By comprehensively covering data access and management, the book guides you through the essential process of setting up your database context and implementing CRUD operations. Equipping you with these skills ensures that your applications not only meet functional requirements but also handle data efficiently and securely.

Security, undeniably, is paramount in today's digital landscape. ASP.NET Core provides sophisticated tools for authentication and authorization, enabling developers to implement secure logins and role-based access controls. We'll delve into these topics, ensuring you understand how to protect sensitive information and maintain user trust, which is essential for any successful application.

Beyond the back-end, integrating modern front-end technologies is crucial for delivering a rich user experience. ASP.NET Core's support for JavaScript, CSS, and even single-page applications allows developers to craft visually appealing and interactive interfaces. The seamless integration of these technologies means you can create cohesive and compelling applications without the need for extensive context-switching between technologies.

No discussion on development would be complete without addressing testing and debugging. Quality assurance is imperative, and knowing how to effectively write unit tests and use debugging tools fortifies the reliability and functionality of your application. We'll explore these techniques, providing concrete strategies to identify and rectify issues before they reach production.

In the world of modern applications, the deployment process can often determine success or failure. That's why ASP.NET Core simplifies deployment with various options, including cutting-edge cloud services. Whether deploying to an on-premises server or leveraging the scalability of cloud platforms, this book will guide you through every step necessary to ensure a smooth rollout of your applications.

Performance optimization often distinguishes good applications from great ones. From caching strategies to load balancing and scaling techniques, you'll learn how to maximize your application's responsiveness and throughput. These optimizations ensure your application remains available and performant under varying loads, making it a central component of your strategy for growth and user satisfaction.

In conclusion, the path to mastering ASP.NET Core is not merely about technical proficiency.

It's about embracing a philosophy of continuous learning and improvement, applying solid principles, and adapting to new challenges with confidence and creativity. Whether you're charting new territories into web development or enhancing your existing skills, this book is your companion on a journey to becoming a proficient and innovative ASP.NET Core developer.

Chapter 1: Getting Started with ASP.NET Core

Embarking on your journey with ASP.NET Core opens up a landscape of flexible and high-performance web development possibilities. Whether you're stepping into the .NET ecosystem for the first time or honing skills in an exciting new direction, ASP.NET Core offers unparalleled advantages in building scalable applications. Getting started means setting up a solid development environment and understanding how ASP.NET Core fits into the broader .NET ecosystem. This stage serves as your foundation—a crucial platform where powerful productivity tools, intuitive APIs, and a supportive community converge to amplify your coding prowess. With each line of code, you won't just be creating applications; you'll be crafting enduring solutions ready to meet tomorrow's challenges with confidence and agility. So get ready, because mastering ASP.NET Core will profoundly transform the way you approach web development, making your concepts evolve from vision to reality in exciting new ways.

Setting Up Your Development Environment

Embarking on your journey with ASP.NET Core starts with establishing a robust and efficient development environment. This foundation is crucial, as it not only supports your initial steps but also scales with your growing ambitions, whether you're crafting small personal projects or expansive, enterprise-level applications. Setting up your development environment correctly ensures you maximize productivity and minimize frustrations. Let's delve into how you can create an optimal setup for ASP.NET Core development.

To get started, you'll need to install the .NET SDK, a suite of tools designed to aid developers in building applications. The .NET SDK includes the .NET CLI, which provides a powerful command-line interface to facilitate tasks like creating, running, and publishing applications. If you haven't installed it yet, head over to the official .NET website, where you can download the latest version. Always opt for the Long-Term Support (LTS) releases for greater stability and support.

Beyond the SDK, selecting the right Integrated Development Environment (IDE) is paramount. Visual Studio and Visual Studio Code are two popular choices for ASP.NET Core. Each has its strengths. Visual Studio offers a comprehensive suite of development tools with built-in debugging, testing, and support for services like

Azure. It's the heavyweight champion that's got everything a developer might dream of. On the other hand, Visual Studio Code, a lighter and nimbler option, is beloved for its versatility and rich extension ecosystem. Its minimalistic interface doesn't skimp on power, and its open-source nature encourages continuous improvement through community efforts.

After selecting an IDE, you might consider customizing it to match your workflow. Most IDEs, including Visual Studio and Visual Studio Code, support a plethora of extensions that can aid ASP.NET Core development. From productivity boosters and code analyzers to theme customizers and version control integrations, the options are numerous. Experiment with a few but remember, while extensions can enhance your workflow, too many can also bloat your environment and slow you down. Strike a balance that offers efficiency without sacrificing performance.

Another fundamental component of your development environment is version control. Integrating a source control solution like Git ensures that you can manage your application's evolution efficiently. Not only does it safeguard your code base with robust backup and recovery options, but it also facilitates collaboration if you're working in a team setting. Platforms like GitHub, GitLab, or Bitbucket provide cloud-based repositories that offer additional collaboration tools and continuous integration pipelines.

Once the basics are in place—SDK, IDE, and version control—consider the operating system you're working on. ASP.NET Core is cross-platform, running on Windows, macOS, and Linux. This flexibility means you can choose an OS that best fits your needs. Historically, Windows has been the go-to for .NET development, but macOS and Linux options have matured significantly due to .NET Core's evolution. Depending on your environment and specific requirements, you might prefer the familiarity of Windows or opt for the robustness of Unix-based systems.

With the core tools installed and configured, don't overlook the importance of maintaining your development environment. Regular updates for your SDK and IDE are crucial. Updates often bring not just security patches but also new features and improved tools that keep your development process both current and efficient. Equally, staying abreast of community-driven extensions and plugins can lead to discovering invaluable tools that aid in streamlining daily tasks.

In creating an ASP.NET Core application, testing is an integral part of the development lifecycle. Therefore, incorporate testing frameworks such as xUnit or NUnit into your environment right from the start. This proactive integration facilitates a test-driven development approach, encouraging you to build resilient, high-quality applications. Testing tools ensure you catch potential issues early, thus avoiding costly fixes later in the development cycle.

As you forge your path as an ASP.NET Core developer, remember that learning never stops. Your development environment will evolve as new practices emerge and your skills grow. Continuously refine your setup by seeking feedback from peers, engaging with the developer community, and experimenting with new tools and extensions. Developing an ASP.NET Core environment is a combination of leveraging powerful tools and tailoring them to your personal workflow, setting you up for success and efficiency.

Ultimately, setting up your environment is about finding what works best for you. It's a blend of personal preference, technical requirements, and adaptability. Remain mindful that your environment should assist you in writing clean, efficient code, and empower you to solve complex problems. With the right setup, you'll be well on your way to mastering ASP.NET Core, ready to tackle whatever challenges come your way.

Exploring the .NET Ecosystem

As you embark on the journey of mastering ASP.NET Core, it's essential to understand the broader .NET ecosystem. With its vast array of libraries, frameworks, and tools, .NET offers developers a comprehensive playground for creating everything from simple web applications to complex enterprise-grade solutions. Whether you're starting your first project or looking to deepen your expertise, immersing yourself in the .NET landscape is key to unleashing the full potential of ASP.NET Core.

The .NET ecosystem is a treasure trove filled with various components and functionalities designed to integrate seamlessly. You'll encounter foundational elements like the Common Language Runtime (CLR), which provides a managed execution environment for .NET code. The CLR handles crucial tasks such as memory management and exception handling, ensuring that your applications run efficiently and reliably. Working alongside it is the Base Class Library (BCL), which offers a vast collection of reusable types and functionalities that simplify everyday coding tasks.

One of the most exciting aspects of .NET is its versatility. The ecosystem supports multiple languages such as C#, F#, and Visual Basic, allowing developers to choose the language they're most comfortable with. C#, in particular, stands out due to its powerful features and optimal performance, making it the preferred choice for many ASP.NET Core developers.

Beyond languages, the ecosystem includes a rich set of frameworks, each with its unique capabilities. For example, ASP.NET Core itself is part of this tapestry, offering a cross-platform, high-performance framework for building modern web applications. On the other hand, Xamarin extends your capabilities further into mobile application development, allowing you to share code across Android and iOS platforms.

Moreover, the introduction of .NET 5, now evolved into .NET 7, marked a significant step in unifying the ecosystem. It simplified the choices for developers by providing a single platform for all types of applications — from Windows desktop to cloud-scale services. This unification aids in reducing complexity and fostering a more efficient development process by eliminating the need to switch between different .NET flavors.

.NET's strength also lies in its expansive library of third-party tools and packages available via NuGet. Whether you need to add data access layers, implement complex UI components, or streamline continuous integration, there are countless packages on NuGet to meet your demands. This wealth of resources not only accelerates development but also empowers you to focus more on solving business-specific problems rather than getting bogged down by repetitive tasks.

For those invested in continuous learning and staying current, the .NET ecosystem welcomes you with an active community and a plethora of learning resources. Forums, blogs, official documentation, and community-driven resources provide a constant stream of information and updates. Engaging with this vibrant community can significantly enhance your skills and keep you abreast of the latest trends and best practices.

An integral component of this ecosystem is its commitment to open-source development. Many parts of .NET, including ASP.NET Core, are open-sourced on platforms like GitHub, inviting contributors worldwide to collaborate and innovate. This transparency fosters a collaborative environment where new ideas can flourish, and you, as a developer, can observe and even participate in the evolution of key technologies.

While exploring the ecosystem, you'll also discover that .NET is deeply integrated with Azure, Microsoft's cloud computing platform. This integration allows for seamless deployment and scaling of applications, leveraging Azure's extensive cloud services. Understanding this synergy is crucial as cloud technologies become increasingly prominent in modern software development.

Lastly, it's essential to mention .NET's commitment to staying cutting-edge. Microsoft continuously invests in improving and expanding the ecosystem, adding new features, and ensuring it meets the demands of contemporary development challenges. As a result, .NET remains competitive and relevant, providing developers with tools and frameworks that evolve alongside technological advancements.

In summary, diving into the .NET ecosystem is more than just a prerequisite for mastering ASP.NET Core — it's an invitation to become part of a dynamic community and an innovative culture. By understanding and leveraging this ecosystem, you're positioning yourself to create robust, scalable, and modern applications that not only meet today's demands but also prepare you for the challenges of tomorrow.

Chapter 2: Understanding ASP.NET Core Architecture

Diving into the heart of ASP.NET Core, we encounter its innovative architecture—built to foster efficiency, modularity, and adaptability. At the core is the simplicity of a unified environment that seamlessly integrates with modern development tools and workflows. ASP.NET Core makes abundant use of middleware, a brilliant concept that allows for flexible request handling through a pipeline of components. This pipeline can be tailored to include essential processes, from authentication to response formatting, each neatly encapsulated in its piece of middleware. Moreover, the architecture embraces dependency injection, a powerful mechanism that simplifies component management and testing. This fosters an ecosystem where developers can craft robust applications with improved maintainability and testability, boosting both individual productivity and team collaboration. Understanding this architecture doesn't just illuminate how ASP.NET Core functions but inspires confidence in building scalable, high-performance applications that truly harness the potential of .NET innovations.

Middleware Components

Middleware is the unsung hero of ASP.NET Core. It's a crucial aspect you need to understand if you want to build responsive, scalable applications. In essence, middleware components are the building blocks of the request-processing pipeline in an ASP.NET Core application. They stand as intermediaries in the path of sorts, each capable of handling HTTP requests and responses.

You can think of middleware as a chain of command. Each component in this chain has two options: it can either handle the request and respond immediately, or it can pass the request down the line. What's fascinating is the level of control these components offer. They can modify both incoming requests and outgoing responses, effectively shaping user interaction. This means that every single request your application receives can be individually tailored, logged, or even blocked if necessary.

When configuring middleware, order matters—a lot. The sequence in which middleware components are added in your pipeline dictates the flow. Imagine it this way: each middleware component has the potential to impact every subsequent component. If you place authentication middleware early, for instance, you can ensure that only authenticated requests get processed further down the chain. It's just like setting up security checkpoints in a building.

Adding middleware to your ASP.NET Core application is straightforward with the `Use` methods provided in the `Startup` class. Functions like `UseRouting`, `UseEndpoints`, and `UseAuthorization` are common players in the middleware setup. Each serves its unique purpose, ensuring requests are routed appropriately, endpoints are executed, and authorization procedures are enforced. It's these subtle yet powerful functionalities that make middleware indispensable.

Creating custom middleware is another thrilling possibility. You're not confined to built-in components; you have the freedom to build specialized middleware to meet your app's unique requirements. The process is simple yet powerful—you define what happens to the HTTP context within your component. Whether it's handling custom headers or performing complex logging, the world is your oyster. Custom middleware can revolutionize your pipeline, making it as robust or as specialized as you need it to be.

Error handling is one area where middleware truly shines. Instead of scattering error handling code across various controllers or services, you can centralize it within a specific middleware component. This not only makes maintenance easier but also ensures that error handling is consistent across the application. Middleware like `UseExceptionHandler` manages such tasks elegantly, providing a valuable safety net.

Middleware also excels at managing cross-cutting concerns, things like logging, authentication, and session management. These concerns are often needed across many parts of a web application, and middleware allows you to address them once, neatly tucked away in the request pipeline. The DRY principle—Don't Repeat Yourself—fits perfectly here. Implementing cross-cutting concerns as middleware components saves both time and thousands of lines of duplicate code.

The flexibility offered by middleware does come with a caveat: with great power comes great responsibility. It's imperative to evaluate the impact of adding each middleware component. Overloading your pipeline with too much middleware can lead to performance bottlenecks, making it essential to consider your application's overall design and requirements. Always aim for a balance between necessary functionality and the performance cost it incurs.

For aspiring developers aiming to master ASP.NET Core, getting comfortable with middleware is crucial. It's the intricacies of middleware that differentiate good applications from great ones. Debugging becomes simpler, and scalability issues become easier to address when you've harnessed this powerful tool effectively. Understanding the flow of the request lifecycle and being mindful of your middleware's configuration are skills that will pay dividends in your development journey.

Finally, as you delve deeper into middleware, remember that you're not alone. The ASP.NET Core community thrives on collaboration; numerous forums and resources can aid your learning process. Explore, experiment, and don't be afraid to dive into the depths of your middleware stack. Each adjustment you make, each custom component you implement adds another layer to your expertise, bringing you one step closer to mastery of ASP.NET Core.

Dependency Injection in ASP.NET Core

The foundation of modern application development in ASP.NET Core is its emphasis on modularity and configurability. At the heart of this design paradigm lies Dependency Injection (DI), a technique that enhances the flexibility and testability of your application by promoting loose coupling between components. Dependency Injection is not just a feature in ASP.NET Core; it's a fundamental part of the framework's architecture. Understanding how to effectively leverage DI can transform the way you develop applications, making your code more maintainable and scalable.

In essence, Dependency Injection is a pattern where a class or object receives other objects that it depends on, instead of constructing them internally. This inversion of control is a critical shift from traditional programming, where dependencies are usually hard-coded within a class. With dependency injection, your application becomes easier to manage, adapt, and test because each component is injected with its required resources from an external source—a process that ASP.NET Core manages seamlessly.

One significant advantage DI brings to ASP.NET Core applications is enhanced testability. When components are no longer tightly bound to the specific implementations of their dependencies, unit testing becomes straightforward. You can easily replace any dependency with a mock or a stub during testing. This helps you isolate the component under test, allowing for more granular unit tests that can verify functionality without the need for external dependencies like databases or web services.

ASP.NET Core makes it incredibly straightforward to implement Dependency Injection. It comes with a built-in, highly configurable, yet simple intuitive service container that registers the service dependencies. Functions like `ConfigureServices` in the `Startup.cs` file allow you to define how dependencies should be resolved. You can register services with various lifetimes—transient, scoped, and singleton—based on your application's need. This built-in DI container supports both constructor injection and, to a lesser extent, method and property injection, facilitating the registration and consumption of services with minimal fuss.

Understanding the different service lifetimes is crucial. Transient services are created each time they are requested. These are ideal for lightweight, stateless services with no need for caching or shared resources. Scoped services, on the other hand, are created once per request in a web application. This is typically used for services that hold state during a single request. Finally, singleton services are created the first time they are requested, or when `ConfigureServices` is run, and every subsequent request uses this cached instance. Choosing the appropriate lifetime for your services ensures the optimal use of resources, enhancing both performance and reliability.

Configuring Dependency Injection in ASP.NET Core is flexible. The `ConfigureServices` method allows you not only to add and bind your application services but also to configure intricate service dependencies. ASP.NET Core's DI container provides flexibility with a hierarchical approach. There's default support for constructor injection but ASP.NET Core's extensible architecture means that you can plug in third-party containers such as Autofac, Ninject, or others if your application has more complex DI needs.

The modular structure of DI in ASP.NET Core fits perfectly with its middleware pipeline. Middleware components that handle requests and responses can also have dependencies injected into them. This means middleware can easily use services registered in the DI container without worrying about how the dependencies are provisioned. It encapsulates the logic that varies independently and considers it as a replaceable aspect of your application that you can swap out seamlessly.

But beyond the technical merits, Dependency Injection fosters a culture of best practices and clean code principles. By naturally encouraging developers to think in terms of interfaces and abstractions, DI contributes to a codebase that's easier to read and less prone to changes that ripple across the entire application when modifications are required. This aligns well with the service-oriented nature intrinsic to ASP.NET Core's design, promoting a separation of concerns and allowing each component to focus on a specific responsibility.

However, mastering Dependency Injection goes beyond merely understanding its mechanics. It requires a deeper appreciation for software design patterns and clean coding principles. As you integrate DI into your ASP.NET Core projects, you'll find that the abstract nature of interfaces makes your code resilient and adaptable. Resilience here means that services can be changed, upgraded, or replaced without impacting the functionality that depends on them.

Looking further, dependency injection promotes reusability. When written well, services you develop can be reused across different projects or components. This can substantially reduce the time spent on developing new applications since the existing, well-tested code can be brought to bear on new challenges.

Despite its many benefits, Dependency Injection requires thoughtful implementation. Not all objects need to be injected, and overuse can lead to confusion and unnecessary complexity. Sometimes new developers can be tempted to inject every possible dependency to cover all potential needs. It's essential to strike a balance, ensuring dependencies are relevant and necessary, so the code remains intuitive and maintainable over time.

In closing, Dependency Injection in ASP.NET Core is an invaluable tool for any developer's arsenal. Its ability to bring about more maintainable, testable, and scalable applications should not be underestimated. As you harness the power of DI, think of it as constructing a robust foundation upon which your application's architecture will be built. By embracing these principles, you are not only enhancing your productivity but also paving the way toward a future where adapting and scaling your software involves confident and deliberate steps.

Chapter 3: Building Your First ASP.NET Core Application

Embarking on the journey of building your first ASP.NET Core application is both an empowering and exhilarating experience. The process kicks off with creating a basic web app, a foundational step that transforms ideas into interactive, scalable applications. By immersing yourself in this task, you're not just writing code; you're crafting the backbone of modern web solutions. Picture yourself seamlessly configuring your development environment, where every line of code becomes a stepping stone towards proficiency. Running and debugging your application will reveal the inner workings of ASP.NET Core, presenting opportunities to refine and optimize as you navigate. Remember, each challenge you face is a chance to grow your expertise. Your first application is the canvas where you'll master the craft, laying the groundwork for more sophisticated projects that lie ahead.

Creating a Basic Web App

Embarking on the journey of building your first ASP.NET Core application starts with creating a basic web app. While it may seem daunting at first, this process is an opportunity to harness the powerful features of ASP.NET Core. By the end of this section, you'll have a functional web app as a foundation to build upon.

Creating a basic web app in ASP.NET Core begins with selecting the right project template. Visual Studio offers a variety of options, but here, we'll focus on the ASP.NET Core Web Application template. This template provides a solid starting point with the necessary files and a predefined structure to kick off your development process. By choosing this template, you seamlessly integrate essential components and structures which enhance your development efficiency.

Once you've selected the template, it's time to configure your project. You'll be prompted to choose a framework version—opt for the latest, stable release of .NET Core to take advantage of the latest features and security improvements. Additionally, you'll decide whether to use HTTPS. Although optional, enabling HTTPS is highly recommended to ensure secure communication. This is a critical step as secure connections are becoming a standard expectation for modern web applications.

With your project configuration set, you're ready to dive into the code. The default template sets up a minimal yet functional sample application. The file structure you'll encounter is organized logically. The "wwwroot" folder is where static files like CSS, JavaScript, and images reside. The "Pages" or "Views" folder, depending on your choice, will house the dynamic content of your application. Understanding your project's layout is critical, as this aids navigation and future scalability of your application.

Now, let's examine the startup process. In any ASP.NET Core application, the `Startup` class plays a pivotal role—it sets up services and the app's request pipeline. Take a moment to explore this class. At first glance, you'll notice methods like `ConfigureServices` and `Configure`. These methods are instrumental in configuring your app's services and middleware. Knowing where these configurations occur will empower you to modify and extend your app with ease.

The `ConfigureServices` method is where you register services with the dependency injection container. Whether you're injecting custom services, setting up Entity Framework Core, or adding authentication, it all begins here. Meanwhile, the `Configure` method defines the request-handling pipeline and is responsible for setting up essential middleware components like routing, static file serving, and error handling. Mastering these methods will allow you to customize the behavior of your application fully.

This basic web app will serve a simple "Hello, World!" page. Observing how ASP.NET Core handles routing is insightful. In the sample project, pages are usually routed through conventions set within the `Startup` class or using attribute routing. As you expand your application, understanding these routing mechanisms will enable you to build complex, user-friendly URL structures.

Running your application for the first time is always an exciting milestone. With ASP.NET Core's built-in Kestrel web server, you can launch your app directly from Visual Studio. Simply hit F5 or click on the green arrow button. Your default web browser will open, displaying your running application. This straightforward process not only validates your setup but also provides a sense of accomplishment.

At this point, your application might seem simplistic, yet its potential for growth is vast. Every feature of ASP.NET Core is built with scalability in mind. As your confidence grows, you'll explore adding new features and functionality, such as integrating database access, implementing authentication, or even building APIs. This initial project lays down the groundwork for experimenting with these advanced concepts later.

As you grow more familiar with ASP.NET Core, don't hesitate to explore its vast resources. The ASP.NET Core documentation is a goldmine for troubleshooting challenges or uncovering best practices. Community resources, forums, and open-source projects can further expand your understanding. Engage actively with these learning opportunities, and your skills will undoubtedly deepen.

Remember, every line of code you write during this process adds value to your skills as a web developer. Building your first ASP.NET Core application is a journey of growth and discovery. There's a world of possibilities at your fingertips ready for you to explore.

By completing this chapter, you've taken your first steps toward mastering ASP.NET Core, setting a foundational understanding upon which you will build sophisticated, scalable applications. Each project you undertake will refine your expertise, bringing you closer to becoming a proficient and innovative web developer in the ever-evolving digital landscape.

Running and Debugging Your Application

Embarking on the journey of running and debugging your ASP.NET Core application is an exhilarating step in your development adventure. It's like piloting a freshly built ship through uncharted waters; here, you'll finally see the fruits of your coding efforts come to life and tackle issues that might arise. In this section, we'll guide you through the essential process of executing your application and delve into the strategies for debugging to make sure your application runs flawlessly. Your goal is to ensure users experience a seamless and polished product.

Once you've constructed your basic web app, the next logical step is to run it. Start by opening your IDE, whether you're using Visual Studio, Visual Studio Code, or any other favored environment. To kick off your application, you'll typically utilize the built-in web server, Kestrel, which provides a lightweight and efficient setup suitable for development and testing contexts.

Running your application in Visual Studio couldn't be simpler. Just press F5, and your application will be built and launched in Debug mode. Visual Studio's IIS Express is utilized here, enabling you to test your application locally with minimal configuration. For those using Visual Studio Code, the process is similarly straightforward. With the .NET Core CLI, you can execute `dotnet run` from your terminal, launching your application using the Kestrel server. This flexibility allows you to decide where and how to run your application.

Now, let's talk about IIS Express and Kestrel. While Kestrel is lightweight and suitable for local testing, IIS Express simulates a more production-like environment. It's essential to test in varying scenarios to ensure compatibility and performance across configurations. Get accustomed to using the appropriate tools for the task, whether it be for development or eventual deployment.

Once your application is running, you'll want to test its functionality across different browsers. This is where cross-browser testing becomes crucial. Each browser may render your output slightly differently due to rendering engines. Testing across these ensures your application meets users' expectations regardless of their choice of browser.

But what happens when things go awry? Debugging. This is your chance to put on your detective hat and solve the mysteries of dysfunctional code. Visual Studio offers a robust set of tools for debugging. Breakpoints are your starting point; they allow the execution to pause, letting you inspect variables and control flow line-by-line. Navigate your code with these tools to uncover bugs, logical errors, or unexpected behavior.

Another invaluable tool in your debugging toolkit is the immediate window in Visual Studio. This feature allows you to query your code while it's stopped at a breakpoint. For instance, you can modify variable values or call functions on the fly, all without altering the source. This flexibility can expedite the bug-fixing process significantly.

Let's not forget about logging, a staple in every developer's toolkit. ASP.NET Core boasts robust logging capabilities that allow you to write diagnostic messages to various outputs. Configure logging to an appropriate level, whether it be Information for general messages or Debug for detailed troubleshooting data. This logging foundation provides an excellent trail to follow when unexpected issues arise in production environments.

When the problems are intricate, inspect your application's asynchronous operations. Debugging asynchronous code introduces additional complexity since operations may not execute sequentially. The Call Stack window in Visual Studio can help unravel this complexity, showing you the hierarchy of calling methods.

Beyond Visual Studio, other debugging options exist if you're using Visual Studio Code or prefer the command line. The .NET Core CLI itself has built-in functions for debugging. You can issue commands that allow you to run your application with attached debugging processes, affording you a comprehensive view of how your application behaves under different scenarios.

Remember, debugging isn't just about fixing errors. It's about learning and understanding your application's behavior in-depth. It's a skill that hones your ability to write clean and efficient code. Take pride in refining these skills; they form the backbone of dependable application development.

Finally, it's important to maintain a cycle of testing and debugging throughout your development process. Regular checks help catch bugs early before they escalate into larger issues. Incorporate automated tests where possible, running them frequently to ensure new code meets existing expectations without breaking current functionality. The continuous integration of testing and debugging not only improves your application's quality but also enhances your coding discipline.

By mastering the art of running and debugging your ASP.NET Core application, you empower yourself to produce not just functioning code but exceptional code. Explore these tools with curiosity, and don't hesitate to experiment in your development environment. You're building not just an application but the expertise to tackle challenges and build solutions that make a difference.

Chapter 4: Routing and URL Management

As you step into the world of routing and URL management in ASP.NET Core, you unlock the potential to create intuitive and user-friendly web applications. Routing serves as the backbone for request handling, mapping incoming URLs to the corresponding application endpoints. In ASP.NET Core, it's the dynamic duo of middleware and routes that empower developers to forge organized paths through their applications. With great flexibility, you can configure simple or complex route patterns, implementing clean URL structures that enhance both search engine optimization and user experience. Realigning URLs using advanced routing techniques like attribute routing and route constraints enables you to dictate application logic intuitively. Master these skills, and navigating the web of possibilities with ASP.NET Core becomes second nature, propelling your projects into the realm of scalable and efficient modern web applications.

Configuring Routes in ASP.NET Core

In the world of ASP.NET Core, routing is the silent architect behind the scenes—an unassuming yet pivotal player that organizes and directs your application's traffic. It serves as the GPS for web requests, ensuring each one reaches its intended destination. By defining the routes, developers can precisely map URLs to their corresponding actions and resources within the application. This mapping is crucial for creating meaningful and user-friendly URLs, which not only improve user experience but also assist with SEO.

Configuring routes in ASP.NET Core starts with understanding the routing middleware. Middleware is a fundamental aspect of ASP.NET Core, acting as the building blocks of the request pipeline. Routing comes into play through this middleware by intercepting incoming requests and determining the path they should take. The correct configuration of this routing can make or break the capabilities of your application in efficiently handling user interaction.

Routes are generally defined in the `Startup` class, specifically within the `Configure` method. Here, the routing middleware is added to the request processing pipeline. You typically start by calling `UseRouting()` to enable routing capabilities. This method sets the stage for configuring routes using controllers, Razor Pages, or other endpoints. Once you've set up the middleware, you can define the routes themselves to control the flow in your application.

ASP.NET Core offers a flexible routing system by allowing you to use some pre-defined patterns or create custom ones. A common structure comprises a combination of controllers and actions with optional parameters, usually structured as `/controller/action/{id?}`. This basic pattern can be expanded or restricted based on specific application needs. The optional parameter `{id?}` means that the presence of the id value is optional, offering versatility in how URLs are structured and used.

There's also attribute routing, which gives you more control over the endpoint URLs directly at the controller level. By using attribute routing, you can decorate your controller actions with routing attributes that define precise paths. This approach allows for greater flexibility as developers can explicitly state routes without being constrained to a single global pattern. It enhances clarity as routes stay close to the code they map to, making the application easier to navigate and maintain.

While defining routes, you need to keep in mind the consideration of route priorities and conflicts. ASP.NET Core resolves routes based on their order of definition. Routes that appear first in the configuration file are tried first, which is why you should place more specific routes before more generalized ones to ensure the correct processing. It's a prioritization strategy that's both simple and powerful, influencing how routes are selected.

Furthermore, ASP.NET Core routing supports route constraints that enforce rules on route parameters. Constraints such as data types, regular expressions, and custom constraints ensure that only valid requests reach your controllers. For instance, if a route parameter has to be an integer, you can apply a constraint that filters any non-numeric values. Understanding these constraints can significantly refine how routes are processed, improving application reliability and safeguarding against errant data.

In multi-language applications, you might need routes to adapt based on the language or culture settings. ASP.NET Core's routing can handle localization features by integrating with globalization middleware or by using custom parameter conventions. This empowers developers to cater URLs and content dynamically based on user location, and it's crucial for applications with a global audience.

Route configuration can be tested to ensure accuracy and functionality. Tools such as logging middleware allow you to output detailed information about how routes are matched and processed. This kind of transparency during development and debugging phases helps developers catch routing errors early, minimizing potential disruptions once the application goes live. Logging middleware thus acts as an indispensable companion during the development lifecycle.

Additionally, remember that URLs and routes don't just have an endpoint function; they also communicate your application's structure and purpose. Descriptive and consistent URLs are vital for reinforcing your brand and providing a seamless user experience. URL construction and management through careful routing choices play directly into this overarching narrative, as they lay the groundwork for intuitive and accessible web navigation.

Collaboration with other teams, such as design and content, is integral during routing configuration. Their input might shape route design to ensure it aligns with user expectations and SEO strategies. A well-executed routing plan can transform your application from just functional to highly intuitive and efficient, embodying a harmony between backend capabilities and frontend experiences.

In conclusion, mastering the configuration of routes in ASP.NET Core equips you with the precision needed to guide every web request to its rightful place. It's this art of defining clear, efficient, and robust routes that succinctly capture the intent of your application's architecture while inviting users to explore its depths. Engaging in mindful routing practices isn't merely a step in the development process; it's about crafting a journey for every user interaction. And in doing so, you build applications that are not only effective but also elegant and user-centric.

Advanced Routing Techniques

Routing in ASP.NET Core isn't just about directing incoming requests to the appropriate endpoints. It's a sophisticated mechanism that can profoundly impact the scalability, maintainability, and performance of your web applications. As you dive into advanced routing techniques, you'll discover how to leverage the full power of routing to create more dynamic and flexible web applications.

At its core, routing in ASP.NET Core is all about patterns and conventions. These patterns dictate how URLs map to the code that processes requests. But what if your project demands something beyond simple mapping? Enter advanced routing techniques, which provide the tools to define routes that adapt to various scenarios, handle complex URL structures, and maintain cleanliness in your application architecture.

First, let's explore the concept of attribute routing, an intuitive and declarative approach where routes are defined directly on action methods using attributes. This method contrasts with conventional routing, which relies on centralized route configuration. With attribute routing, you gain the ability to make your routing closely align with your application structure. It facilitates self-documenting code and provides granular control over how routes are defined at the action level. For instance, you can quickly adjust parameters, constraints, and defaults directly at the point of action definition, making your codebase easier to understand and maintain.

Attribute routing shines in applications requiring fine-tuned control over URL generation. Imagine constructing an API where you need specific endpoints to reflect a logical organization of resources. By using attribute routing, each action method can have a unique route, helping maintain clear and concise routes without the spaghetti-code risk. However, it's crucial to balance this with centralized route configuration to prevent route conflicts and duplication.

Another game-changer in advanced routing is route constraints. Constraints allow you to match URLs based on more than just the pattern format. This means that routes can be filtered by HTTP method, domain, or even based on a custom logic inside a constraint class. For example, you could ensure that a particular route only matches if a segment resembles an integer or a valid date format. This level of precision reduces errors and increases the robustness of your application by ensuring that only valid requests reach the appropriate handlers.

Speaking of custom constraints, creating them opens doors to meet specific project requirements that the built-in constraints can't handle. The custom route constraints enable you to define sophisticated checks directly in the routing mechanism, thereby reducing the workload on your controllers. This separation of concerns is beneficial because it leads to cleaner and more maintainable code.

Then there is the power of route templates and parameter transformers. With route templates, you can design routes that are both consistent and predictable. Parameter transformers, on the other hand, let you manipulate route values as they are converted into URLs. For instance, you could convert a parameter value into a different case style (e.g., camelCase or kebab-case), ensuring that the URLs generated by your ASP.NET Core application follow your desired naming conventions. This ability to tweak URL outputs without altering the actual route definitions is invaluable when maintaining a consistent and SEO-friendly URL format.

When dealing with larger projects, consider endpoint routing, which decouples route matching and execution. It treats routes as first-class elements across middlewares, thus enabling advanced scenarios like middleware-based authorization. Through endpoint routing, ASP.NET Core allows precise execution paths and provides a foundation for enhanced performance optimizations. This strategy is increasingly adopted for its flexibility and control, giving you fine-grained access to middleware and maximizing performance through reduced overhead.

Let's not forget the importance of route priorities and order. Being intentional about the order in which routes are evaluated is crucial, as

ASP.NET Core processes routes sequentially. The first matching route will handle the request. A carefully structured route setup helps to avoid unintentional overrides and ensures that the most specific routes are matched first. This approach maintains performance while still offering flexibility.

Finally, localization in routing is an indispensable advanced technique for applications that cater to global audiences. By integrating culture-aware URL generation and matching, you ensure that your application's routes are naturally adaptable to different languages and regions. Localization enhances user experience and ensures that the URLs remain intuitive and accessible to a diverse audience.

In summary, mastering advanced routing techniques is fundamental to elevating your ASP.NET Core applications. By employing attribute routing, custom constraints, parameter transformers, and endpoint routing, you gain the ability to refine and enhance the routing system's power and flexibility. These techniques equip you to create more dynamic applications that meet intricate business requirements while remaining maintainable and scalable. Embrace the possibilities of advanced routing, and your applications will not only be functionally superior but will stand as elegant examples of well-structured web development.

Chapter 5: Working with Razor Pages

As we dive into Razor Pages, it's important to appreciate their unique power in turning web page design into a seamless and efficient process. Razor Pages offer a focused, page-centric alternative to the traditional MVC framework, which keeps both novice and seasoned developers in mind. By using Razor Pages, you're able to streamline your coding efforts, which ultimately enhances productivity and project coherence. Their simplicity lies in binding logic to pages directly, ensuring that you keep your focus where it matters most—on the content and user interaction. This approach not only disciplines your development workflow but also fosters an intuitive way to harness razor syntax for dynamic content generation. Armed with these tools, you're well-equipped to craft web applications that are both robust and easy to maintain. Embracing Razor Pages is more than just a stylistic choice; it's about evolving as a developer and leveraging the potential that ASP.NET Core offers.

Creating Razor Pages

Razor Pages, introduced in ASP.NET Core as a simple yet powerful way to create page-focused scenarios, offer a streamlined approach for building web apps. As you embark on creating Razor Pages, it's crucial to understand their structure and the benefits they bring to your development toolkit. While traditional ASP.NET MVC requires controllers and views, Razor Pages condense these into a single, cohesive unit, making your development process more intuitive.

Imagine starting with a blank canvas. Razor Pages simplify this by reducing the cognitive overhead associated with managing both a controller and a view. At its core, a Razor Page combines the structure of a view with the logic of a controller into a page model, a plain old C# class embedded within a page. This effectively keeps the code behind tightly culminated with the UI, leading to better maintainability and clarity.

To get started, you need to create your Razor Pages within an ASP.NET Core project. Begin by setting up a project, choosing the Razor Pages template. This template pre-configures the fundamental necessities, such as a layout and some pre-baked pages for navigation, to jumpstart your development. You'll notice a folder structure under the Pages directory; each .cshtml file represents a Razor Page, backed by a PageModel class in a .cshtml.cs file. Here lies the beauty of Razor Pages—everything pertinent to a page lives in its folder, making code organization a breeze.

The PageModel file, being the beating heart of your Razor Page, deserves your attention. It contains handlers—methods that respond to HTTP requests for the page. Understanding these handlers is pivotal as they determine the kind of logic that can be embedded directly into your page, from basic GET and POST to richer custom HTTP verbs. This mechanism is a departure from traditional models of serving requests, but it is exactly this divergence that provides developers with powerful new ways to streamline their application workflows.

Here's an example: If you're building a subscription form, the logic for serving and processing the form can be handled right within a single context using these handler methods. Your GET requests can prepare the form, while POST requests can validate and process the data—tidily encapsulated within the same model. This feature allows you seamless synchronization between UI and server-side logic, a hallmark of Razor Pages.

Creating your first Razor Page starts with understanding the anatomy of a Razor Page file which is split into three simple parts. First, there's the directive section at the top of the .cshtml file, where you'll typically find an @page directive marking the file as navigable via a URL. Next is the HTML and Razor syntax block. Here,

Razor syntax excels at weaving C# code into HTML, offering you dynamic content rendering with minimal effort. Lastly is the backend PageModel class that binds your data, manages interactions, and handles HTTP requests seamlessly.

No discussion of Razor Pages would be complete without exploring its powerful data binding capabilities. Razor Pages support two-way data binding, meaning that not only can you display bound data, but changes to input elements can automatically update the data model. This process is initiated through Tag Helpers, robust snippets that produce server-side rendered HTML dynamically. Tag Helpers, such as asp-for, are instrumental in bridging server data with UI elements.

Moreover, one of the quintessential benefits of Razor Pages is their support for routing. The @page directive tells Razor where to route requests and can even accept route parameters directly in the page model. This feature reduces the complexity of managing external routing configurations, letting you define routes more organically within the context of each page. Consequently, navigation becomes more intuitive from both a development and a user perspective.

It's essential for developers to leverage Razor Pages to craft better user experiences by making applications responsive and engaging. The combination of easy integration between frontend and server-side logic results in faster development times and cleaner, more maintainable code. As you think about building scalable, efficient, and user-friendly applications, Razor Pages present themselves as a compelling option.

As you explore further into Razor Pages, remember that its design philosophy emphasizes simplicity without sacrificing capability. The structure of Razor Pages inherently leads to cleaner, more organized solutions, and the all-in-one-page model syncs content with logic in a way that's intuitive and accessible, even for those new to ASP.NET Core. This newfound simplicity doesn't negate the need for best practices and thoughtful architecture but offers a framework conducive to modern web app development.

With Razor Pages in your toolkit, the next step is to experiment and explore. Let your creativity guide the design of your applications, revel in the practicality of this innovative approach, and watch as the code you write does more with less, right from the jump. In the journey to mastering ASP.NET Core, the knowledge of crafting Razor Pages will undoubtedly be one of your most valuable tools.

Using Razor Syntax for Dynamic Content

Diving into the world of Razor Pages, one of the most compelling features you'll encounter is Razor syntax for dynamic content creation. At its core, Razor is a simple yet powerful templating language embedded within ASP.NET Core. It lets developers infuse C# code directly into HTML, enabling dynamic web page rendering in an intuitive and efficient manner. This seamless integration allows developers to construct interactive and data-driven web applications without breaking a sweat.

Razor syntax is concise, using the `@` symbol as a trigger to switch between HTML and C#. This elegant design minimizes the cognitive load on developers as they seamlessly merge backend logic with frontend content. Dynamic interpolation becomes more than just a technical function—it becomes a tool for crafting exciting user experiences. Whether you're retrieving data from a server to display user-specific information or integrating complex data structures into your page layout, Razor syntax lets you do it all with flair and ease.

One of the first encounters with Razor syntax is likely within expressions, wherein a simple line like `@DateTime.Now` can dynamically pull the current date and time into your webpage. These expressions aren't limited to just outputs; they can perform operations as well, such as conditional statements or loops, much like you'd expect in C#. For instance, using a `@foreach` loop, developers can iterate over collections, creating list elements dynamically based on data—ideal for displaying items like product catalogs or user listings.

Let's not overlook Razor's ability to conditionally display content. With conditional statements such as `@if`, `@else`, and `@switch`, developers wield the ability to control which blocks of HTML are rendered based on certain conditions. Think about a situation where you want to display a message welcoming users back upon login, but only if they have recently logged in. This can be simply achieved with Razor syntax, providing a personalized touch to user interaction.

Moreover, Razor syntax shines when it comes to layout management. It allows developers to define reusable components using partial views or layout pages. This is crucial in maintaining a consistent look across various pages while ensuring that dynamic content can still be managed effectively. Imagine creating a blog page where the header and footer remain the same, but the content in between changes depending on the blog post. This modularity enhances both the maintainability and scalability of your application.

Beyond standard programming constructs, Razor brings its own set of directives that provide additional functionality. For example, the `@functions` directive enables you to define helper methods directly in your Razor view, granting you the power to keep view-specific logic neatly encapsulated. Then there's the `@model` directive, a cornerstone of Razor Pages which facilitates strong typing. With the `@model` directive, Razor pages can directly bind to models, enabling seamless data flow between your application and the frontend.

However, with great power comes the need for careful management. Since Razor syntax allows embedding C# within HTML, it's essential to maintain a clear separation of concerns. Overstuffing your Razor pages with logic can lead to messy and hard-to-maintain code. Ideally, complex logic should be delegated to backend services, keeping the Razor view clean and focused solely on presentation.

Security, too, plays a critical role when using Razor syntax. While Razor does a great job of sanitizing output to prevent cross-site scripting (XSS) attacks, developers should always be mindful of the data sources and apply comprehensive security practices, such as data validation and encoding, to safeguard their web applications. The integrity and security of a dynamic application are paramount.

Developers should capitalize on Razor's strengths by regularly updating their skills and exploring advanced features through continuous learning. Engaging with the community, reviewing the latest updates, and experimenting with new patterns and practices can illuminate novel ways of leveraging Razor's capabilities. It's about pushing the limits to discover just how interactive and exciting your ASP.NET Core projects can become.

In conclusion, mastering Razor syntax in ASP.NET Core isn't just about learning to use a set of tools—it's about finding creative ways to build powerful, dynamic applications. Harness its ability to blend C# logic with HTML to seamlessly deliver personalized and real-time content. As you explore Razor further, you will find it isn't just a feature of ASP.NET Core; it's a launchpad into becoming a more adept and innovative web developer. Your journey with Razor Syntax is a key chapter in your ASP.NET Core narrative. Embrace it wholeheartedly, and watch your projects come to life in vibrant new ways.

Chapter 6: Controllers and Views

As we continue our journey into the depths of ASP.NET Core, it's time to dive into the realm of Controllers and Views, the beating heart of the Model-View-Controller (MVC) pattern that ASP.NET Core embraces so gracefully. Controllers serve as the traffic directors of your application, routing data and requests between the user and the server, while views provide the visual magic that turns data into an interface a user can interact with. Together, they form a cohesive duo that allows developers to build web applications that are not only robust but also elegantly structured. Navigating the intricacies of Controllers and Views, you'll find yourself gaining mastery over how an app processes and displays information. This understanding paves the way for crafting experiences that are both dynamic and responsive. So, let's step into this chapter and explore how Controllers and Views empower developers to craft scalable and maintainable web applications with confidence and control.

Implementing MVC Pattern

The Model-View-Controller (MVC) pattern stands as a pillar in ASP.NET Core architecture, offering a clean separation of concerns that boosts both maintainability and scalability. By dividing an application into three interconnected components—Model, View, and Controller— developers can manage complexity and promote organized code structures. The MVC pattern aligns well with modern software development practices, empowering developers to create applications that are both efficient and flexible.

At the heart of the MVC pattern lies the Controller. It's the conductor of your application, orchestrating the flow of data and determining how user requests are handled. When a request comes in, the Controller receives it, processes any necessary information, and decides which View should be presented back to the user. This centralized control makes it easier to manage and update application logic without having to trawl through multiple layers of code.

Controllers in ASP.NET Core are typically classes that inherit from the Controller base class. They're designed to handle HTTP requests, process user inputs, and interact with models to retrieve or manipulate data. Actions, implemented as methods within Controllers, respond to HTTP verbs (GET, POST, etc.) and define what each endpoint can do. By utilizing attributes like [HttpGet] or [HttpPost], you can specify precisely which action method should respond to a given HTTP request. This clear demarcation of responsibilities simplifies both the understanding and expanding application capabilities.

The Model, another crucial player in the MVC architecture, represents the data layer of your application. It encapsulates the business logic and data access logic, ensuring that these concerns remain segregated from UI and input handling. Models are typically implemented as classes or interfaces that can work seamlessly with a database through technologies like Entity Framework Core. This approach not only promotes reusability but also enhances testability, as you can mock or stub out Models when writing unit tests, free from UI constraints.

Views are responsible for rendering the user interface and displaying data to the end-users. In ASP.NET Core, Views are typically created using Razor, a dynamic template engine. Razor Views contain HTML combined with C# code, giving you a powerful yet straightforward way to generate dynamic content. This blend of markup and logic allows developers to have direct control over the HTML output without resorting to cumbersome and error-prone manual string concatenation methods common in other technologies.

A View in the MVC framework doesn't handle any logic. Instead, it relies on data passed to it from the Controller—often in the form of a ViewModel. ViewModels serve as the intermediary between the Model and the View, transferring data while abstracting and shaping the Model data according to the needs of the View. By using ViewModels, developers gain the flexibility to include additional information that may not directly map to the Model, therefore tailoring the data more explicitly to the View's requirements.

The beauty of the MVC pattern is evident when changes are needed. If, for example, a business rule changes, you only need to update the respective Model or Controller without touching the View. Similarly, redesigning the user interface doesn't necessitate changes to the way data is fetched or processed. This separation of concerns means different parts of an application can be developed in parallel, improving efficiency and reducing potential for conflicts among developers.

When implementing the MVC pattern in ASP.NET Core, routing is crucial. ASP.NET Core employs a robust routing system to map incoming requests to Controller actions. This system allows developers to define custom routes, supporting everything from simple convention-based routes to complex, attribute-based routing strategies. As a result, the MVC pattern offers considerable flexibility in defining how web requests are directed through your application's infrastructure.

The MVC pattern encourages a test-driven development environment, enhancing the reliability and quality of applications. Because Controllers, Models, and Views can be tested independently, developers are equipped to catch and resolve issues early in the development cycle. Unit and integration tests become more straightforward, allowing developers to exercise the business logic in isolation of the UI. This emphasis on testing not only cultivates better code practices but also fortifies the application against unexpected runtime errors.

Though MVC is incredibly powerful, it's essential to be mindful of its complexities. Over-engineering is a common pitfall, where developers may unnecessarily complicate a solution by adhering too rigidly to the pattern. As with any architectural approach, it strikes a balance between structure and simplicity—using the MVC components where they naturally fit while acknowledging that certain scenarios may warrant different patterns or a blend of approaches.

ASP.NET Core's implementation of MVC is a testament to its maturity and capability as a web framework. It promotes a standardized way to build robust, scalable applications that are easier to maintain and extend over time. By adhering to the MVC principles, developers are positioned to tackle complex projects without sacrificing clarity or quality, ensuring that efforts invested today benefit your application's future evolution. Ultimately, mastering the MVC pattern in ASP.NET Core not only makes you a proficient developer but also a more effective problem solver in the vast landscape of modern software development.

Managing Views and ViewModels

In the world of ASP.NET Core, the Model-View-Controller (MVC) pattern stands as a pillar for building robust web applications. The "Views" and "ViewModels" play a crucial role, particularly at the interface where users interact with your application. Understanding how to effectively manage Views and ViewModels sets apart a seasoned web developer from a novice. Let's dive into the essentials of creating dynamic, user-friendly, and maintainable views through smart use of ViewModels.

To begin with, Views in ASP.NET Core are responsible for rendering the user interface. They are the visual components that users touch and feel. Views are typically represented by Razor files (.cshtml) that harness HTML capabilities augmented with Razor syntax for embedding server-side logic and data. Although Views are dumb in terms of logic, they are intelligent enough to present data engagingly. This concept of minimal logic in Views ensures that the business logic and user interface remain separate, each attending to its dedicated responsibilities without stepping on each other's toes.

While Views are the abstraction level where users interact, ViewModels serve a different purpose. They act as a bridge between your data (Models) and Views. ViewModels are specially crafted objects that hold the data and state needed by a View. They can aggregate data from multiple sources, bringing together exactly what is necessary to meet the View's display requirements. With a well-designed ViewModel, you can keep your View's code cleaner and less cluttered, as all the data manipulation and formatting can be handled within the ViewModel.

Consider this analogy: if Views are actors in a play, then ViewModels are the scripts. They tell the actors not just what to say, but reflect the precise mood and intonation required. By carrying detailed information about the data context, ViewModels ensure that Views get precisely what they need for their roles without having to improvise. This separation of concerns reduces complexity and increases code maintainability.

The advantage of using ViewModels is not just about neatness, but also about flexibility. ViewModels can be tailored to the needs of specific scenarios. Need to display a list of data along with user feedback? Create a ViewModel that encapsulates both the list and feedback properties. This approach minimizes dependencies on the domain models, allowing your application's data layer to evolve independently of its interface layer.

Developing effective ViewModels requires a mindset shift. Start thinking in terms of what data a page should present and how that data is structured. When building your ViewModel, consider the data fields that the View will require. Define properties in your ViewModel that correspond to data you want to display or collect from the user. Also, include any formatting or transformation logic that might be necessary to adapt raw data into a more suitable format for presentation.

Binding Views to ViewModels is straightforward in ASP.NET Core. In your controller action method, populate a ViewModel instance with data from your domain models or services. Then, pass this ViewModel to the View. When using strongly-typed Views, define your ViewModel type at the top of your Razor file using the `@model` directive. This gives you access to the ViewModel properties via IntelliSense, allowing for a seamless development experience. For instance:

@model MyApp.ViewModels.ProductViewModel

@Model.ProductName

@Model.Description

This seemingly simple approach has powerful implications. By decoupling View logic from database models, you have the freedom to refactor both layers independently. Suppose you need to refactor your database model. With ViewModels in place, you merely need to update how data is fetched or mapped, leaving your UI logic untouched.

A common pattern is to define dedicated ViewModel classes for each distinct View. This encompasses the Single Responsibility Principle, ensuring each ViewModel has one job—to satisfy a specific View's needs. Keep in mind that even if two Views require overlapping data, crafting separate ViewModels is often better than a shared approach. This not only enhances code readability and maintainability but also aligns with how views are rendered and interacted with, ensuring each page or component has a dedicated and clear context.

Testing becomes more straightforward with ViewModels, too. By encapsulating presentation logic within a class, you can unit test ViewModels, ensuring that data formatting and management logic function as intended. This boosts the quality of your application and confidence in code changes or enhancements.

As your application grows, managing Views and ViewModels efficiently can turn into an art. Adopting practices like view-model binding, validation, and mapping libraries can further streamline development. Libraries such as AutoMapper can facilitate the mapping of complex domain models to leaner ViewModels, enhancing productivity and reducing boilerplate code.

The challenges of balancing View complexity with readability are ever-present. Strive to avoid logic-heavy Views; instead, entrust your ViewModels to carry the load. If a ViewModel becomes bulky, consider if it's trying to do too much. Break it down into smaller, more focused pieces that promote clarity and focus.

Moreover, ViewModels offer a great place for validation logic. Using data annotations, you can define rules that ensure data correctness before it ever hits your database. This adds another layer of defense against invalid data entry, safeguarding both your application's integrity and user experience.

When designed and implemented correctly, Views and ViewModels complement each other like a well-choreographed dance. They combine to deliver fast, responsive, and reliable web applications. Embrace their potential, and you pave the way for an architecture that not only meets current requirements but is poised for future advancements.

Empower your applications by embracing this separation of concerns while fostering a strong bond between data and presentation. The clarity and efficiency gained will ripple through your development process, ushering in applications that stand the test of time, ready for whatever challenges come next.

Chapter 7: Data Access with Entity Framework Core

Entity Framework Core (EF Core) is the bridge that brings together the ease of database interaction and the power of ASP.NET Core, allowing you to weave data access seamlessly into your applications. It's not just about connecting to a database; it's about doing so with elegance and efficiency. With EF Core, you can define a database context that represents the bridge to your databases, catching and manipulating data with precision. As you dive deeper, you'll find CRUD operations becoming as natural as writing a simple method. EF Core empowers you to shape data models that are as agile as your application requires, facilitating changes with minimal friction. The marvel of EF Core lies in its ability to abstract and simplify, making data-driven development not just a task, but a skill that adds a robust layer to your development toolkit. You'll find motivations in its flexibility whether you're spinning up a quick prototype or crafting a large-scale enterprise solution. Embrace this powerful tool and see your productivity soar, as you effortlessly manage data flow within your ASP.NET Core applications.

Setting Up Your Database Context

In the world of modern web development, data is king. To effectively access and manipulate data, one must skillfully wield a powerful tool, and in the realm of ASP.NET Core, Entity Framework Core (EF Core) is just that tool. Let's dive into one of the fundamental steps in leveraging EF Core: setting up your database context.

To start with, understanding the role of the `DbContext` class is crucial. At its core, the `DbContext` in EF Core acts as a bridge between your domain or business logic and the database. It's not just a set of APIs for querying the database; it's an abstraction that allows you to interact with the database in a more intuitive way using the language of your business domain. Think of it as your application's translator, converting high-level operations into database queries.

Before you can set up the `DbContext`, you need to ensure your project has the necessary references. EF Core requires specific NuGet packages. Typically, you'd install `Microsoft.EntityFrameworkCore` and a provider for your database. There are various providers like `Microsoft.EntityFrameworkCore.SqlServer` for SQL Server, or `Microsoft.EntityFrameworkCore.Sqlite` for SQLite. Choose based on your specific database needs.

Once you've got your NuGet packages in place, it's time to configure the `DbContext`. Begin by creating a class that derives from `DbContext`. This class will act as a blueprint for your database, specifying entities and their configurations. You'll create properties for each data model you want to include as a `DbSet`, which are typed sets representing the tables in your database.

csharp

```csharp
public class ApplicationDbContext : DbContext

{

public DbSet Products { get; set; }

public DbSet Customers { get; set; }

}
```

In the example above, `ApplicationDbContext` includes `DbSet` and `DbSet`, representing tables for products and customers. The `DbSet` type provides a lot of functionality, including querying and saving instances of T, which translates to rows in the database.

Configuration of the context continues in the `OnConfiguring` method or through the ASP.NET Core Dependency Injection system's `AddDbContext` method. For applications following modern best practices, it's common to use dependency injection to set up the context. In your `Startup` class (or `Program` class in newer .NET versions), you'll add your context to the service container, specifying the connection details.

csharp

```csharp
public void ConfigureServices(IServiceCollection services)

{

services.AddDbContext(options =>

options.UseSqlServer("YourConnectionStringHere"));

}
```

This is a pivotal moment. The connection string is your application's access point to the database. It's crucial to get it right — not just to ensure connectivity but also considering security implications, as it often contains sensitive information like usernames and passwords.

Mapping configurations are also an essential part of setting up your context. EF Core provides conventions for how entities are mapped to database schemas, but sometimes you'll need explicit configurations. This can be achieved using the Fluent API or Data Annotations. Embedding these configurations in your `OnModelCreating` method allows you to refine how entities map to databases, define relationships, or enforce validation rules.

```csharp
protected override void OnModelCreating(ModelBuilder modelBuilder)

{

modelBuilder.Entity()

.HasKey(p => p.ProductId);

modelBuilder.Entity()

.Property(p => p.Name)

.IsRequired()

.HasMaxLength(100);

}
```

These configurations ensure your database schema aligns perfectly with your application's needs. They also enhance data integrity and enforce business rules directly within your database context setup.

Finally, let's touch upon migrations, which are a lifesaver for database version control. Once your context is configured, migrations allow you to apply changes incrementally to the database schema. Use the command-line interface or package manager console to add, remove, or update migrations, and apply them to your database with ease and confidence.

```bash
```

```
dotnet ef migrations add InitialCreate
```

```
dotnet ef database update
```

By setting up your database context correctly, you lay a strong foundation for all database operations in your application. Mastering this process empowers you to effortlessly interact with databases, seamlessly bridge code and data, and ultimately build robust, scalable web applications with ASP.NET Core. As you move forward, remember that this setup is not merely a technical necessity; it's an opportunity to align your data access approach with your application's architecture, facilitating maintainability and performance.

CRUD Operations with EF Core

CRUD—short for Create, Read, Update, and Delete—is the backbone of any data-driven application. EF Core simplifies these operations, allowing developers to interact with databases without delving deep into complex SQL syntax. It's about focusing on the business problem at hand, rather than worrying about repetitive data access code. Let's dive into how EF Core facilitates CRUD operations in your ASP.NET Core applications.

Create: Adding data to your database is often the first step in any CRUD interaction. With EF Core, creating a new record is straightforward. First, you'll instantiate a new entity, populate its properties, and then add it to the relevant DbSet. This is done through the *Add* method. Finally, calling *SaveChangesAsync* will commit these changes to your database. While this sounds simplistic, it's precisely how EF Core abstracts the common tasks to let you focus on more critical areas of development.

For instance, imagine a simple scenario where you have a *Product* entity. Here's a quick representation of how you'd create a new product:

```csharp
var newProduct = new Product { Name = "Laptop", Price = 1500 };
```

```csharp
_context.Products.Add(newProduct);

await _context.SaveChangesAsync();
```

This bit of code tells EF Core: "Here's a new product. Please save it to the database." Behind the scenes, EF Core translates this to a SQL *INSERT* command. This simplicity allows developers to focus on what's important: building features that deliver value.

Read: Reading data is ubiquitous across applications, from displaying user profiles to listing products. EF Core's LINQ integration makes it immensely powerful. LINQ, or Language Integrated Query, lets you write queries within the comfort of your C# syntax. These queries are then translated by EF Core into the corresponding SQL queries for execution.

Whether you're fetching a single entity or retrieving a list, EF Core makes it intuitive. Consider fetching a product by its ID:

```csharp

var product = await _context.Products.FindAsync(productId);
```

What if you want a list of all products priced above $1000? With EF Core, that looks like this:

```csharp

var expensiveProducts = await _context.Products
```

```csharp
.Where(p => p.Price > 1000)

.ToListAsync();
```

EF Core allows for advanced querying capabilities, yet keeps the process intuitive, ensuring developers can work effectively without getting bogged down in complexity. This empowerment is critical when building scalable applications.

Update: Updating existing records is a frequent requirement. With EF Core, you load the entity, modify the property values, and then save the changes. EF Core's change tracking automatically detects which values have changed and will generate the appropriate *UPDATE* statements.

Here's how you might update a product's price:

```csharp
var productToUpdate = await
_context.Products.FindAsync(productId);

if (productToUpdate != null)

{

productToUpdate.Price = 2000;

await _context.SaveChangesAsync();

}
```

Updating data with EF Core feels natural and seamless. Its internal mechanisms ensure that only modified data is updated, optimizing what's sent to the database.

Delete: Removing data from a database is another primary operation. With EF Core, once you've identified the entity you want to delete, you can remove it using the *Remove* method, followed by another call to *SaveChangesAsync*.

Consider deleting a product:

```csharp
var productToDelete = await _context.Products.FindAsync(productId);

if (productToDelete != null)

{

_context.Products.Remove(productToDelete);

await _context.SaveChangesAsync();

}
```

EF Core has always strived to make complex operations as straightforward as possible. By focusing on the entity you wish to remove, developers can avoid the intricacies of constructing and executing delete commands manually.

CRUD operations with EF Core are all about giving you power and simplicity in the same package. These operations are foundational, yet they don't shackle you to database specifics. You work with domain classes, and EF Core handles the underlying data interactions. This approach not only boosts productivity but also fosters an environment where developers can innovate without constraints.

While EF Core handles the bulk of data access concerns, understanding its features and quirks ensures even greater productivity. Things like handling concurrency, managing relationships, and leveraging migrations are part and parcel of creating robust applications. EF Core's approach to CRUD — balancing ease of use with powerful capabilities — is an essential cog in the wheel of Asp.NET Core development.

Chapter 8: Authentication and Authorization

Diving into Authentication and Authorization in ASP.NET Core means equipping your applications with the security they need to flourish in the digital age. By strategically implementing these features, you're not just safeguarding your app—you're empowering it to reach its fullest potential. This chapter tackles the essentials, guiding you through a variety of authentication strategies that align with your application's needs. With a definitive look at role-based access control, you will learn how to assign and manage roles, ensuring users interact with only what they should. Whether you're crafting an application for a small startup or a robust enterprise solution, these foundational elements will help you create secure and scalable platforms. Keep the user's trust at the forefront, and your efforts will lead to successful, resilient solutions that stand the test of time. This knowledge arms you to be not just a developer, but a guardian of your web applications.

Implementing Authentication Strategies

When it comes to implementing authentication in ASP.NET Core, being strategic is paramount. Authentication isn't just a technical requirement; it forms the foundation for ensuring your applications can securely manage user identities. ASP.NET Core offers a rich toolkit for building robust authentication solutions, and getting the basics right sets the stage for success. In this section, we'll break down some key strategies you need to build secure and reliable applications. Each strategy comes with its unique advantages and serves different types of applications, so understanding them is critical.

To kick things off, let's dive into the simplest form of authentication: cookie-based authentication. It's a classic approach known for its ease of use. The beauty of cookie authentication lies in its simplicity and the seamless user experience it offers. Once a user logs in, ASP.NET Core issues a cookie that can travel with subsequent requests, allowing the server to recognize the user and manage sessions effectively. Leveraging the built-in Cookie Authentication Middleware, developers can implement security controls with minimal fuss. It's incredibly handy for traditional web apps where the user communicates directly with the server for each request.

Token-based authentication, on the other hand, is tailored for modern applications, particularly those needing to communicate with various servers or services. Here, JSON Web Tokens (JWTs) shine. JWTs are compact and self-contained, making them a convenient choice for single-page applications and scenarios involving distributed systems. Storing user claims and metadata within the token, JWTs can be verified without needing server-side storage, which is a game-changer for stateless applications. Integrating JWT authentication in ASP.NET Core involves configuring the JWT Bearer Middleware, but once set up, it opens up a world of secure API communications.

OAuth 2.0 and OpenID Connect represent more complex strategies but offer comprehensive solutions for modern authentication needs. They are standards that allow third-party services, like Google or Facebook, to authenticate users in your application. OAuth 2.0 is primarily about authorization, letting users grant third-party services access to their resources without sharing credentials. OpenID Connect builds on OAuth 2.0, adding authentication layers. ASP.NET Core's integration with these protocols is robust, allowing applications to tap into a wealth of user data and third-party applications seamlessly. It's particularly beneficial for applications that need a federated identity solution.

For enterprise applications, Windows Authentication is a staple and is particularly preferred in intranet environments. ASP.NET Core leverages existing Windows accounts for automatic user authentication, obviating the need for managing passwords. This strategy is tightly integrated with the Windows operating system, making it straightforward for environments using Active Directory. It ensures that user authentication is both secure and streamlined, fitting seamlessly into enterprise security architectures.

Another consideration in implementing authentication strategies is the use of IdentityServer. It stands out for its approach to building OpenID Connect and OAuth 2.0 compliant applications. Particularly suitable for cases where you need a custom authentication server, IdentityServer provides the flexibility to manage user authentication across applications and APIs alike. Implementing IdentityServer can initially seem daunting due to its complexity, but the power and flexibility it offers make it a cornerstone for scalable and secure applications on ASP.NET Core.

ASP.NET Core Identity is the default membership system for handling users, passwords, profile data, roles, claims, tokens, etc., and it integrates seamlessly with most authentication strategies. It provides a useful abstraction layer for managing user data and offers a pluggable system that allows customization to meet unique security requirements. With built-in support for two-factor authentication, account confirmation, and other security features, ASP.NET Core Identity should often be your go-to choice for applications that require detailed identity management without overly complex integrations.

Security isn't just about choosing an authentication method; it's about tailoring each strategy to suit specific application needs. Factors like where and how your application is deployed, the type of users, and the data access requirements will guide you in selecting the proper strategy or combination of strategies. In ASP.NET Core, hybrid approaches are often adopted to leverage the strengths of different authentication mechanisms. For example, combining cookie authentication with OAuth 2.0 can capitalize on the simplicity of cookies while embracing the flexibility and features of OAuth.

By now, it should be clear that implementing authentication strategies in ASP.NET Core involves careful consideration and planning. Developers must weigh the pros and cons of each method against their specific needs. Cookie authentication might offer simplicity, but JWTs offer flexibility for mobile applications. OAuth 2.0 and OpenID Connect bring potential for wide integration but add complexity. Windows Authentication provides seamless integration within enterprise environments but is less applicable for public-facing applications.

Documentation, testing, and ongoing management are as crucial as the initial implementation. Each authentication strategy requires a detailed understanding, from setup through to maintenance, ensuring that long-term goals are met without compromising security or user experience. Using methods like logging and monitoring can help identify issues and improve security postures over time.

Ultimately, mastering authentication and authorization in ASP.NET Core sets you up for creating applications that not only serve their purpose but do so securely and effectively. The tools and frameworks provided by ASP.NET Core are both sophisticated and powerful, enabling you to craft solutions that align with your vision and users' needs. Choose wisely, code diligently, and adapt as necessary to ensure that your authentication strategies scale alongside your applications, providing peace of mind for both developers and users alike. Embrace these methodologies, and your path toward creating secure and resilient applications with ASP.NET Core becomes that much clearer.

Role-Based Access Control in ASP.NET Core

Role-Based Access Control (RBAC) is a cornerstone of application security, allowing developers to define access permissions based on user roles rather than individual user accounts. In the context of ASP.NET Core, this approach provides a flexible and scalable method for managing authorization logic, ensuring that users access only what they're permitted to. Let's dive into the mechanics of configuring and implementing RBAC to keep our applications secure and maintainable.

The fundamental idea behind RBAC is simple yet powerful: different roles possess different levels of access within an application. ASP.NET Core leverages this concept by allowing developers to assign roles to users and restrict or allow access to resources based on these roles. Utilizing the framework's built-in authentication and authorization middleware, we can manage roles and permissions effectively.

Configuring role-based access in ASP.NET Core typically begins with setting up identity and authentication. ASP.NET Core Identity is a popular choice for managing users, passwords, roles, and more. It provides an out-of-the-box solution for handling authentication, after which you can easily add roles to the mix. Start by adding ASP.NET Core Identity services to your solution in the `Startup.cs` file, within the `ConfigureServices` method. Here, you can specify options for password strength, lockout settings, and even set up the role services necessary for implementing RBAC.

Roles in ASP.NET Core can be assigned straightforwardly. Once you've configured ASP.NET Core Identity, creating and managing roles in your application becomes a task of interacting with the role manager and user manager services provided by Identity. Typically, you'd create roles during the application's initial setup, assigning them to users either through an admin interface or programmatically during development.

Once roles are defined, applying them to controllers and actions is the next step. The `[Authorize]` attribute in ASP.NET Core allows you to specify roles required to access a given resource. By decorating your controllers or actions with this attribute, you can enforce role-based restrictions smoothly. For example, applying `[Authorize(Roles = "Admin")]` to a controller method ensures that only users in the "Admin" role can execute that action. This fine-grained control helps maintain the integrity and security of your application.

Sometimes, there's a need for more advanced logic than simple role checks. ASP.NET Core provides policy-based authorization, which compliments RBAC by allowing developers to define custom authorization rules. Policies can encapsulate complex access logic and can be associated with roles. By defining policies in the

`Startup.cs` file and applying them using the `[Authorize(Policy = "YourPolicyName")]` attribute, you can achieve a higher level of control over who gets to do what in your application.

Testing role-based access configurations is crucial to ensuring your security measures work as intended. Utilizing unit and integration tests, developers can verify that roles and policies are enforced correctly. ASP.NET Core's testing framework supports numerous testing strategies, and mocking role assignments or creating test users with specific roles can help emulate real-world scenarios. Effective testing safeguards your application from unauthorized access while providing confidence in your authorization implementation.

The beauty of RBAC in ASP.NET Core lies in its versatility and power. As applications scale and grow more complex, managing individual permissions can become a nightmare. By leveraging roles, you centralize and simplify your security model. Changes to permissions can be as easy as adjusting a single role's access, making administration and maintenance much more straightforward.

Furthermore, ASP.NET Core's approach to role management extends beyond mere access restriction. It serves as a foundation for additional security measures, such as logging and monitoring of role changes, integration with external identity providers, and support for hierarchical roles where a user might inherit roles and permissions. These capabilities ensure that RBAC in ASP.NET Core is not just about keeping unauthorized users at bay but also about providing an architecture that can evolve alongside your application's needs.

In conclusion, Role-Based Access Control in ASP.NET Core offers a strategy to handle user permissions with elegance and scalability. By assigning roles and tying them to specific resources, developers create a security model that is both powerful and flexible. As you continue to build applications with ASP.NET Core, remembering the principles of RBAC will not only enhance security but will also streamline development and reduce maintenance overhead. Embrace the discipline of role-based access, and it'll serve you well as you write robust and secure web applications.

Chapter 9: Frontend Integration

In the dynamic landscape of today's web development, mastering the art of frontend integration is a key to unlocking the full potential of ASP.NET Core applications. This chapter delves into the seamless incorporation of JavaScript and CSS, crucial elements for creating engaging user interfaces that captivate and respond intuitively to user input. We'll explore strategies for embedding these technologies into your projects, paving the way for a robust foundation that supports single-page applications and more complex setups. By harnessing modern tools and frameworks, you can craft interactive experiences that complement the powerful backend capabilities of ASP.NET Core, ensuring your applications stand out in functionality and performance. The fusion of frontend and backend is not just a technical challenge; it's an innovative journey that transforms ideas into reality, urging developers to push boundaries and redefine what's possible in web applications.

Using JavaScript and CSS in ASP.NET Core

Incorporating JavaScript and CSS into your ASP.NET Core application isn't just about making things look pretty or adding some superficial interactivity. It's about creating a seamless and responsive user experience, blending backend functionality with a polished frontend. You've built your foundation—your application runs, your data flows—but how it feels to the user often hinges on these powerful tools.

ASP.NET Core is inherently flexible, allowing for robust integration with both JavaScript and CSS. Start by understanding how your project structure supports this integration. Typically, your project set up in Visual Studio will include folders specifically for *wwwroot*, where you can place your *js* and *css* files. These serve as static files that are openly accessible and can be updated without rebuilding your application. It's a small yet powerful feature, ensuring your site can remain dynamic and responsive over time.

The separation of concerns is fundamental. By keeping your JavaScript and CSS files logically organized within the *wwwroot*, you maintain clarity and simplify maintenance. When you work with JavaScript libraries, like jQuery or React, you're utilizing scripts to handle client-side logic, making asynchronous calls to your server, and manipulating the DOM. Knowing where your scripts sit in relation to your page's lifecycle is crucial. Therefore, ensure your scripts are strategically placed at the bottom of your HTML or use **async** and **defer** attributes when they're in the head section to prevent blocking rendering.

CSS works hand-in-hand with JavaScript to provide a visually compelling layout. ASP.NET Core projects are often styled with frameworks such as Bootstrap, which can be easily integrated. Including a reference to the Bootstrap CSS file in the layout page or importing it via a CDN can streamline the appearance and behavior of your web components. Remember, encapsulating styles within specific CSS classes prevents conflicts and keeps your markup clean.

Using the *Tag Helpers* introduced in ASP.NET Core for script and style inclusion makes life a tad easier. Consider the *Environment Tag Helper*, which ensures you're loading the correct set of files based on the environment—be it development or production. For instance, minified versions in production reduce loading times, giving users a faster experience. Notably, ensuring CSS and JavaScript are compressed and cached can turn a sluggish app into a snappy one.

Let's also touch on AJAX, a technique that allows for the asynchronous exchange of data between the server and client. This means parts of your web page can update without reloading. In ASP.NET Core, AJAX calls are often employed through the Fetch API or using libraries like Axios. They offer a sophisticated way to enhance user interaction, ensuring data is up-to-date and dynamically rendered.

With JavaScript frameworks such as Angular, React, or Vue.js making headlines, incorporating them with ASP.NET Core becomes a decision of scale and complexity. These frameworks allow developers to build complicated user interfaces with ease. ASP.NET Core's flexibility extends to these frameworks via robust API integration, letting you serve RESTful endpoints while managing front-end interactions elegantly.

Let's not forget testing—an essential yet frequently neglected phase. Tools like Jasmine and Mocha enable you to unit test your JavaScript code, ensuring functionality remains intact throughout development. ASP.NET Core's tight integration with these testing frameworks helps maintain a smooth development process, ultimately resulting in software of higher quality.

In conclusion, integrating JavaScript and CSS with ASP.NET Core adds layers of interactivity and visual appeal to your application that are critical for a modern web experience. The interplay of well-structured front-end scripts and styles with powerful, scalable server-side capabilities creates a holistic development experience. As you progress with ASP.NET Core, remember the goal is not just to make functional apps, but to craft experiences that count. Take pride in mastering these integrations—they are the threads that tie together function and form in your web development endeavors.

Single-Page Application Integration

Integrating Single-Page Applications (SPAs) with ASP.NET Core is a critical skill for building smooth, efficient, and highly interactive web experiences. SPAs are popular for their ability to update content dynamically without reloading the entire page, making web applications feel fast and fluid. ASP.NET Core, with its robust backend capabilities, provides an ideal platform to host and manage SPAs. Whether you're building with Angular, React, or Vue.js, ASP.NET Core offers seamless ways to integrate these frameworks to create cohesive and responsive user experiences.

In an SPA, the key concept is that the application loads a single HTML page and dynamically updates it as the user interacts with the app. Traditionally, web applications involve multiple page loads which can be slower and less efficient, especially if the server has to send the same assets repeatedly. SPAs address this by maintaining a fluid interface where JavaScript frameworks handle routing and view updates client-side. ASP.NET Core acts as a backend service provider that efficiently handles data operations and business logic. By configuring your project intelligently, you can leverage ASP.NET Core's server-side capabilities with the agility of SPAs.

Getting started with SPA integration involves setting up your ASP.NET Core project alongside your chosen JavaScript framework. It's crucial to establish a clear separation between server-side code and client-side assets. This allows both to evolve independently while still communicating seamlessly. You'll typically organize your project to keep the server-side concerns, like API controllers and business logic, distinct from the client-side assets managed by webpack or another build tool specific to your JavaScript framework.

One effective pattern for integrating SPAs into ASP.NET Core is using API-driven development. Your SPA can make HTTP requests to the ASP.NET Core back end to fetch or send data, allowing you to maintain a RESTful or GraphQL service layer. This separation of concerns not only keeps your codebase organized but also sets the stage for potentially scaling your application into different platforms or mobile applications. ASP.NET Core's comprehensive middleware features come into play here, acting as intermediaries to manage requests, enable logging, authentication, and even compress content before it reaches the client.

While working with SPAs, you'll find that cross-origin requests from the client to the server are common. Configuring Cross-Origin Resource Sharing (CORS) in ASP.NET Core is essential to enabling these requests while enforcing security policies. Allowing controlled access from your client-side application to your server-side API ensures that your application remains secure yet flexible enough to handle various client demands. It's about striking a balance between accessibility and security, which ASP.NET Core helps to achieve through its versatile configuration options.

Integrating features like server-side rendering (SSR) is another area where the collaboration between ASP.NET Core and SPAs becomes beneficial. SSR can significantly improve the initial load time of your application by rendering the initial HTML on the server, providing users with a quick and complete view of the application that progressively hydrates as JavaScript takes over. ASP.NET Core's support for SSR can be seen in how it often partners with frameworks like Angular Universal or Next.js in the case of React, delivering enhanced performance and SEO benefits.

The development environment also plays a crucial role. ASP.NET Core offers package templates that support SPA development. These templates can help bootstrap your project, providing a foundation that integrates ASP.NET Core with SPA frameworks. For instance, if you're using Angular or React, there are dotnet CLI commands that can scaffold an ASP.NET Core project pre-configured to work with these frameworks. These templates typically handle dependencies, static files, and development tasks like running both the ASP.NET server and the JavaScript build process collectively, which is particularly useful during development.

It's essential to be aware of the various lifecycle management processes involved when deploying

SPAs alongside an ASP.NET Core application. Building and deploying a single-page application involves packaging your client assets through a build tool, then integrating them into your ASP.NET Core application. The integration usually lands these files in a location from which ASP.NET Core can serve them, like the 'wwwroot' folder. Proper versioning and cache-busting techniques ensure that users always get the latest content without stale data trapped by browser caches.

One seamless experience is achieved through the use of Proxy Middleware in the ASP.NET Core project. While developing an SPA, setting up proxy middleware can route API requests to the backend while serving frontend files from the SPA's development server. This setup provides a simplified development workflow where frontend developers can work on a static file server with hot module replacement while still interacting with the live backend API.

Finally, testing SPAs within ASP.NET Core projects requires attention to detail. Both unit and integration testing can be enhanced by using tools tailored to the SPA framework in question, like Jasmine and Karma for Angular, or Jest and Enzyme for React. When you tie these testing strategies into your ASP.NET Core application, you cover both the client and server sides with rigorous, automated checks that ensure your application remains robust, reliable, and performant.

In the grand scheme of web development, integrating SPAs with ASP.NET Core is about harnessing the strengths of both client-side and server-side technologies. It is about building applications that are not just functional but also engaging and responsive to the user's needs. With careful planning, thoughtful architecture, and a keen focus on performance, SPAs augmented by ASP.NET Core can help shape the future of web applications, providing a pathway for developers to evolve their skills and deliver exceptional digital experiences.

Chapter 10: Testing and Debugging ASP.NET Core Applications

Diving into the crucial aspect of testing and debugging in ASP.NET Core applications can feel empowering, and getting it right is pivotal to ensuring robust software. The art of testing involves crafting unit tests that meticulously validate the functionality of your components, all while maintaining the flexibility to adapt and expand. It's about wielding tools like xUnit and Moq with precision to simulate complex scenarios and handle edge cases. Debugging, on the other hand, demands an analytical mindset, leveraging Visual Studio's exceptional debugging capabilities to trace execution paths and pinpoint elusive bugs. The journey of debugging also encourages the proactive use of logging and exception handling to foresee issues before they arise. Effectively navigating through these processes not only enhances the stability of your applications but also cultivates an innate sense of confidence in your development skills, pushing you closer to mastery in crafting scalable and reliable ASP.NET Core applications.

Writing Unit Tests

Unit testing is a crucial practice for anyone serious about writing maintainable and reliable software. In ASP.NET Core, creating unit tests not only ensures that your code works as expected but also fortifies your application against future bugs when changes are made. The core idea behind unit testing is to test each component of your application in isolation. By doing this, you can pinpoint faulty code quickly without the distractions of a broader system.

When writing unit tests for ASP.NET Core applications, the first tool that generally comes to mind is xUnit. xUnit is a popular unit testing framework for .NET applications and serves as an excellent choice for ASP.NET Core due to its strong community support and comprehensive set of features. One of xUnit's great advantages is its minimalistic syntax, enabling developers to write tests quickly with clear and concise code.

Let's start by examining a simple example. Suppose you have a service in your ASP.NET Core application responsible for calculating discounts. Before any application's logic goes live, you should pepper this service with a suite of tests ensuring it's airtight. Here's how a unit test using xUnit might look:

Imagine a service with a function `CalculateDiscount` that takes in the original price and a discount percentage. You'd write test methods that confirm its output is accurate across varied scenarios.

To effectively set up your testing environment, it's a good practice to keep your business logic decoupled from your controllers and services via interfaces. This design choice not only follows the best practices of dependency injection, a key feature of ASP.NET Core but also paves the way for easy mock implementations during testing. Tools like Moq can then be used to mock these interfaces, which means you can simulate their behavior without having to interact with actual implementations in your tests.

Once you've decided on your testing tools and begun writing your tests, strive to embrace the principles of good test composition. These principles include:

- **Clarity:** Each test should test a single concept or thing. Avoid testing multiple functionalities in one test method.

- **Comprehensive Coverage:** Don't just test for success. Consider the edge cases, the unexpected inputs, and known potential faults.

- **Maintainability:** Keep your tests easily understandable, so future developers (or even you) can comprehend them without difficulty.

Now, consider the importance of using meaningful names for your test methods. A good test name should describe what is being tested, under what circumstance, and what the expected outcome is. This naming convention can make your test suite serve as a form of living documentation for your application's behavior.

Another significant tip while writing unit tests is to ensure that they are quick. The faster your tests, the more frequently you'll run them. Developers are more likely to execute a test suite if it produces nearly instantaneous results. Slow tests, on the other hand, often become an impediment, leading to a situation where tests are skipped more often than not.

Unit tests not only validate your current application logic but also serve as an ongoing check against regressions. Every time you refactor or extend your code, running your test suite should provide the confidence that nothing has broken. This sort of reassurance allows developers to experiment with optimization and improvements without the constant fear of introducing bugs.

Aspiring to writing perfect unit tests may seem daunting at first, but like any skill, it improves with practice. Start with simple tests and gradually advance to testing complex interactions within your application. Remember, the aim is to improve your code's reliability and your confidence in it.

In summary, writing effective unit tests in ASP.NET Core follows a clear path: utilizing well-supported frameworks like xUnit, keeping tests organized and focused, and ensuring that your tests cover a wide range of cases. While the initial learning curve might feel steep, the payoff in application stability and developer confidence is immense. As you become familiar with writing unit tests, you'll find this aspect of development less of a chore and more of a valuable tool in your craft.

Using Debugging Tools Effectively

Getting to grips with debugging is more than just finding bugs; it's about understanding the intricate dance of your application's logic. ASP.NET Core, with its rich set of debugging tools, offers a powerful platform for honing this skill. This section is designed to explore how you, as a developer, can leverage these tools to ensure your applications work flawlessly and efficiently.

Debugging in ASP.NET Core starts with the right environment setup. Microsoft Visual Studio stands out as one of the most effective IDEs for ASP.NET Core development, providing integrated debugging features that streamline the troubleshooting process. With its step-by-step debugging capabilities, you can pause execution to inspect variables and walk through your code line by line. This allows a deeper understanding of what's happening under the hood and helps isolate issues quickly.

One of the essential tools in your debugging toolkit is the breakpoint. By strategically placing breakpoints, you have the power to pause execution at specific lines of code. This pause is your opportunity to examine the state of your application. It's crucial to become proficient in setting conditional breakpoints, which can allow you to stop execution only when certain conditions are met, adding a layer of precision in your debugging process. Instead of sifting through each iteration of a loop, focus on the ones that matter.

The Immediate Window in Visual Studio is another valuable asset. It enables you to evaluate expressions, execute statements, and even change variable values on the fly during debugging sessions. This real-time feedback helps you experiment with fixes before applying them permanently, making it a great tool for hypothesis testing.

If you've ever been puzzled by asynchronous operations not behaving as expected, you're not alone. Debugging asynchronous code can be tricky due to its non-linear execution flow. Tools like Call Stack, Task Window, and Parallel Watch in Visual Studio guide you through asynchronous debugging by allowing you to inspect the hierarchy of active method calls and monitor the state of tasks. These tools untangle async operations, providing clarity on their progression through your application.

As you're debugging, consider leveraging logging as a complementary technique. Logging provides a persistent insight into your application's behaviors and can be invaluable when working with production issues where traditional debugging isn't feasible. ASP.NET Core includes a structured logging system built on ILogger, which you can easily integrate into your application. It enables filtering logs based on their importance, aiding in narrowing down the logs to the most relevant events.

For front-end issues, the browser's Developer Tools is your best friend. Whether it's CSS not rendering as expected or JavaScript throwing unexpected errors, browsers like Chrome and Firefox provide built-in tools to diagnose and resolve such problems. Use features like the Elements tab to inspect and tweak HTML/CSS dynamically, and the Console and Network tabs to catch errors and review HTTP requests and responses.

Remote debugging is an advanced skill you'll find indispensable as applications move from development to staging and production environments. Visual Studio's ability to attach to remote processes brings you closer to understanding how your code performs in environments that mimic real-world scenarios. This is particularly crucial when debugging issues that don't manifest in the development environment. However, it requires careful setup and security considerations, emphasizing the importance of sensible access controls.

Another cornerstone of effective debugging is learning to read and interpret stack traces. When exceptions occur, a stack trace provides a bread crumb trail that reveals the precise path the code took before failing. Familiarizing yourself with interpreting stack traces aids in pinpointing the root cause of errors, especially when combined with detailed logging messages.

For performance-related bugs, profiling tools like the Visual Studio Profiler or third-party tools such as JetBrains dotTrace can be game changers. They help you identify bottlenecks by visualizing CPU usage and memory consumption. Profiling allows you to track down functions that consume resources inefficiently, giving you actionable insights into how you can optimize performance and improve your application's responsiveness.

Learning to use these debugging tools isn't just about acquiring new skills; it's about building a mindset that's relentlessly curious and problem-solving oriented. When effectively utilized, these tools reveal the hidden layers of your application, fostering an environment where your skills can thrive. Approach each debugging session as both a challenge and an opportunity to learn and grow as a developer.

As you continue your journey through ASP.NET Core, remember that mastering debugging tools is key to delivering robust and reliable applications. Equip yourself steadily, experiment tirelessly, and cultivate a meticulous attention to detail. These skills are critical not just for debugging, but also for understanding and crafting better software aligned with your vision.

Chapter 11: Deploying ASP.NET Core Applications

Deploying your ASP.NET Core application is the final stretch of the development journey, where careful preparation meets practical execution. It's essential to ensure that all aspects of your application, from configuration settings to security measures, are fine-tuned for a smooth launch. By exploring various cloud deployment options, you're not just unlocking the potential of scalability and accessibility but also embracing the future of software delivery. Whether it's leveraging Azure for seamless integration or deploying on AWS for robust infrastructure, the choices you make will directly influence your application's performance in the real world. Deployment isn't just about getting your app to run on a server; it's about paving the way for innovation, growth, and an elevated user experience. As you take these steps, remember to monitor, adapt, and thrive, using every tool at your disposal to transform your vision into a living, breathing entity on the web.

Preparing for Deployment

Deploying an ASP.NET Core application is a task that requires meticulous preparation to ensure a smooth and successful launch. It's not just about getting your code onto a server; it's about making sure everything is configured correctly and that the environment can support your application in the long run. Preparation isn't just a step; it's a phase that can determine the success of your deployment. Let's dive into some of the key elements involved in this crucial stage.

First, consider the environment where your application will reside. You'll need to decide on the type of hosting that fits your project's needs, whether that's a traditional server setup, cloud-based infrastructure, or a containerized solution. Each option comes with its peculiarities, advantages, and limitations. Choosing the right one could mean the difference between high performance and a sluggish application.

Next, let's talk configuration. ASP.NET Core is known for its flexibility, and this extends to its configuration system. Before deployment, ensure that configuration files, such as appsettings.json, are correctly set to handle production variables. Utilize environment variables for sensitive data like API keys and connection strings. This not only secures your application but also makes it adaptable to different environments, such as staging and production.

Security shouldn't be an afterthought. Before deploying your application, make certain it's secure by following best practices. This includes implementing HTTPS throughout your application's lifecycle, utilizing secure headers, and validating input wisely to prevent common vulnerabilities like SQL injection and cross-site scripting (XSS). Proper security configurations can protect sensitive user data and prevent unauthorized access, keeping both your application and its users safe.

Don't forget logging and monitoring. Incorporate robust logging to track application activities and diagnose issues efficiently. ASP.NET Core provides built-in logging that can be extended with third-party providers like Serilog or NLog. Couple this with monitoring tools that allow real-time tracking of your application's health and performance. This proactive approach ensures that you can catch and resolve issues before they escalate into user complaints.

Performance is yet another crucial factor. Prior to deployment, run performance tests to uncover bottlenecks within your application. This includes testing database queries, evaluating page load times, and ensuring minimal response times. Performance optimizations such as caching static content and optimizing database calls can make a marked difference in user experience and resource utilization.

Before you hit the deploy button, ensure that continuous integration/continuous deployment

(CI/CD) pipelines are properly configured. A well-implemented CI/CD pipeline automates testing and deployment processes, minimizing the hassle of manually pushing updates and reducing the margin for human error. Tools like GitHub Actions, Azure DevOps, and Jenkins can automate these workflows, enabling faster and more reliable deployments.

Documentation, though often overlooked, is a vital part of the preparation process. Document every aspect of your deployment configuration, from server setups and environment variables to security protocols and emergency recovery procedures. Comprehensive documentation serves as a valuable resource for new team members and can greatly aid troubleshooting efforts when issues arise post-deployment.

Lastly, consider the importance of testing your deployment process itself. Even with thorough preparatory steps, things can still go awry. Conduct a trial run of your deployment procedure in a staging environment that mirrors your production setup. This rehearsal can identify any gaps in your process and ensure that you've tested all components—everything from rolling back in case of failure to scaling when necessary.

In wrapping up, preparing for deployment is an integral stage that touches on various aspects of your web application project. By focusing on the right environment, ensuring correct configuration, securing the application, logging meticulously, optimizing performance, and setting up efficient CI/CD processes, you pave the way for a successful deployment. This ecosystem approach not only safeguards your application but also enhances the overall user experience, empowering you to bring robust solutions to life with ASP.NET Core.

Cloud Deployment Options

In the realm of deploying ASP.NET Core applications, cloud deployment stands out as a transformative force. Cloud computing has reshaped the landscape of web application deployment, serving as a catalyst for unprecedented scalability and flexibility. Let's delve into the diverse cloud deployment options available, offering you a roadmap to leverage the power of the cloud for your ASP.NET Core applications.

Firstly, we have Infrastructure as a Service (IaaS), a foundational layer of cloud computing. IaaS allows you to rent virtualized computing resources over the internet. With services like Microsoft Azure and Amazon Web Services (AWS), developers can deploy full control over their server environment. This option is ideal for those who want to manage the operating system and application installs themselves while benefiting from the cloud's scalability and cost-effectiveness. In this setup, you can optimize resource utilization by deploying multiple instances to handle varying loads efficiently.

Platform as a Service (PaaS) offers another compelling option by abstracting much of the underlying infrastructure complexity. Azure App Services and AWS Elastic Beanstalk are prime examples. PaaS platforms handle OS maintenance, load balancing, and scaling, allowing developers to focus on application logic and functionality. Deploying ASP.NET Core applications on PaaS can significantly reduce the time to market due to simplified deployment procedures. Moreover, these platforms support continuous integration and deployment pipelines, which can accelerate your development cycles and enhance collaboration among teams.

Serverless computing introduces yet another dimension. It's a revolutionary approach where developers don't have to worry about servers at all. Services like Azure Functions and AWS Lambda enable function-based deployment. In a serverless environment, your ASP.NET Core components execute in response to events, making it a perfect match for microservices architectures. This model provides nearly unlimited scaling and billing based purely on execution time rather than pre-allocated resources. It's an optimal choice for scenarios requiring high availability without the hassle of server management.

When considering cloud deployment, containerization has become indispensable. Docker and Kubernetes have evolved as key players in this domain. With Docker, you can package your ASP.NET Core application and its dependencies into a standardized unit, which can run consistently across multiple environments. Pairing Docker with Kubernetes orchestration on cloud platforms, such as Azure Kubernetes Service (AKS) or Amazon Elastic Kubernetes Service (EKS), empowers you to manage deployments, scaling, and operations of application containers at scale.

Hybrid cloud deployment combines on-premises resources with cloud resources, offering a balanced approach. This model is particularly beneficial for organizations with legacy systems that can't be migrated entirely to the cloud. By leveraging tools such as Azure Arc, you can extend cloud capabilities to your on-premises infrastructure. It's a strategic choice when regulatory or compliance requirements demand certain data to remain on-premises, blending the best of both worlds.

As you prepare your application for the cloud, it's vital to adopt cloud-native principles. These principles emphasize designing applications to embrace the dynamic and distributed nature of modern cloud environments. Implementing practices like 12-factor app methodology can improve your application's scalability and resilience. Emphasizing configuration management, stateless processes, and automated testing can greatly enhance your deployment efficiency and reliability.

Security should also be a priority in your cloud strategy. Cloud providers offer robust security frameworks, but it falls upon developers to configure them properly. Utilizing identity and access management services, like Azure Active Directory or AWS IAM, ensures secure access to cloud resources. Moreover, integrating best practices for data encryption and network security fortifies your application against potential vulnerabilities.

Finally, don't overlook the importance of monitoring and performance optimization in cloud deployments. Utilizing tools such as Azure Monitor or AWS CloudWatch can provide critical insights into your application's health and performance. These insights are pivotal for proactively managing resources and ensuring high availability. Setting up automated alerts and performance dashboards can help in swiftly identifying and resolving issues, ensuring your application runs smoothly under varying loads.

In a world where digital experiences define business success, cloud deployment options for ASP.NET Core applications play a pivotal role in driving innovation and efficiency. By harnessing the right mix of IaaS, PaaS, serverless, and containerization, you can ensure your application is not only scalable and efficient but also resilient and adaptive to the ever-evolving technological landscape. The cloud isn't just a destination; it's a journey toward transforming how applications are built, deployed, and experienced.

Chapter 12: Performance Optimization and Scalability

When it comes to crafting web applications that not only function but excel under pressure, performance optimization and scalability become pivotal. As developers, our goal isn't just to make something work; it's to make it work well and sustain that excellence as demand grows. This chapter dives into the art of refining ASP.NET Core applications, enhancing their speed, efficiency, and ability to handle increased loads seamlessly. We'll explore strategies that elevate your application's performance, making it resilient and responsive. You'll discover how effective caching can drastically reduce load times and see how load balancing transforms your infrastructure into a robust, scalable force. By embracing these principles, you're not just reacting to growth; you're preparing for it, laying down a strong foundation that supports your applications now and well into the future. Let's unlock the potential of ASP.NET Core, ensuring your creations not only meet expectations but exceed them as you scale the peaks of modern web development.

Caching Strategies for ASP.NET Core

When it comes to performance optimization and scalability, caching emerges as a powerhouse technique. In the realm of ASP.NET Core, caching isn't just an option; it's a crucial component for ensuring applications remain responsive under load. Caching helps by storing frequently requested data in memory, reducing the need for expensive data retrieval operations on every request. This can lead to significant improvements in application speed and server responsiveness.

The first layer of exploring ASP.NET Core caching begins with understanding the different types available. Broadly, we categorize them into in-memory caching, distributed caching, and response caching. Each of these offers unique capabilities and caters to different needs. In-memory caching, for instance, is optimal for scenarios where data needs to be stored temporarily and quickly retrieved, localized to a single application's space. It's simple and incredibly efficient because it leverages the server's memory.

Distributed caching takes a step further, suitable for applications running across multiple servers. By storing cache data in a shared external store, such as Redis or SQL Server, distributed caching ensures all application instances have access to the same data. Consequently, this technique improves reliability and consistency when dealing with replicated environments. Imagine a scenario where multiple servers are serving requests for the same application. Distributed caching harmonizes the data cache, preventing discrepancies. Sounds powerful, right?

Considering response caching, it uniquely focuses on caching the output of responses returned to clients. This means once a specific request is handled, the server can store that response and directly serve it for identical future requests without reprocessing. It's particularly useful for static content or content that doesn't change frequently. Using response caching, not only do you save processing time but also reduce latency, enriching user experience.

Implementing caching involves more than just choosing the right type. It's about setting the proper policies and strategies. For in-memory caching, the simplicity of storing and retrieving objects using keys can make life easy. Yet, tuning cache size and expiration policies is essential. Too little allocated memory might lead to frequent cache misses, while too much could bloat your application's memory footprint.

Sliding and absolute expirations are your friends here. Sliding expiration resets the time-to-live countdown with each access, perfect for high-use data. Absolute expiration specifies a fixed time at which the data expires, regardless of access frequency. Think of absolute expiration as setting deadlines for your data. What deserves what type of expiration is largely dependent on your application's data access patterns.

The landscape of distributed caching in ASP.NET Core is rich with options. Redis stands out due its speed, reliability, and rich support for various data structures. If you go down this road, ASP.NET Core's integration with Redis is relatively painless, thanks to its out-of-the-box support. Implementing Redis as your caching store demands attention to connection management and handling cache serialization formats. But once set up, you're rewarded with an incredibly fast and scalable caching system.

On the other hand, SQL Server can serve as a distributed cache store, especially welcoming if you're already using it as a primary database. While it might not match Redis in terms of sheer speed for cache retrieval, the trade-off is often balanced by the convenience of leveraging existing infrastructure. Key considerations here include thread management and ensuring the database connections don't become a bottleneck.

Response caching is another strategic piece of the puzzle. It typically involves configuring server headers to specify cache controls and expiration directives. Such configuration can help browsers and proxies understand how to handle cached content. However, response caching can be tricky when your content varies based on headers like language or currency. Varying by headers (using "VaryByHeader" directive) can fine-tune response caching policies, ensuring user-specific results aren't indiscriminately cached.

Think of caching strategies as a toolbox rather than a one-size-fits-all solution. Sometimes, combining different caching techniques—such as using in-memory caching for session data together with response caching for static content—can yield optimal results. The balance often hinges on a clear understanding of your application's workload patterns, server configurations, and data volatility.

Monitoring and evaluating cache performance is paramount. Just because you've implemented caching doesn't mean the job's done. Utilize performance metrics to keep tabs on hit rates and cache efficiency. This vigilance helps you continuously tailor caching mechanisms to your actual usage patterns.

Finally, caching isn't merely a technical concept; it's a mentality. Embracing caching as part of your architecture encourages developers to be creative in reducing redundant data processing. By doing so, you're not just improving performance—you're enhancing your application's scalability. As ASP.NET Core continues to evolve, so too does the caching landscape, presenting ever more sophisticated techniques and tools to harness.

So gear up, explore, experiment, and integrate caching strategies tailored to your specific ASP.NET Core project. With caching well-implemented, you'll be well on your way to delivering fast, resilient, and scalable web applications.

Load Balancing and Scaling Techniques

When building ASP.NET Core applications, one of the critical factors for success is ensuring that your application can handle increasing loads as more users interact with it. That's where load balancing and scaling techniques come into play. These approaches aren't just about keeping your systems responsive; they're about creating an environment where your application can thrive and grow in demand without compromising performance or reliability.

Load balancing is the process of distributing incoming application traffic across multiple servers. It's like having multiple checkout lanes open in a store; if one line gets busy, customers are directed to another open lane, ensuring quicker service. In the same way, load balancing directs traffic to different servers, preventing any single server from becoming a bottleneck and potentially crashing under excessive load.

Various load balancing techniques can be utilized depending on the needs and architecture of your ASP.NET Core application. Round-robin, least connections, and IP hash are among the common strategies. Round-robin is the simplest, where each server in a group gets traffic in turn. Think of it like taking turns on a carousel. This technique is easy to implement but doesn't account for the varying performance capacities of different servers or the state of loads they're currently handling.

For applications requiring more intelligent decision-making, a least-connections approach may be more suitable. In this strategy, incoming traffic is directed to whichever server has the fewest active connections. By doing so, you ensure that requests aren't just evenly spread, but are also directed towards available resources more intelligently, balancing load more effectively than the round-robin approach.

Another sophisticated technique involves IP hashing, where client requests are routed based on a hash of their IP address. This method is particularly useful when you need a sticky session experience; in other words, when the same client must be directed to the same server for session persistence.

Scaling, on the other hand, is all about expanding the capacity of your application to handle increasing traffic. This can be achieved via vertical or horizontal scaling. Vertical scaling, or scaling up, involves adding more resources to your existing servers like CPU, RAM, or storage. This technique can be straightforward, but it's limited by the capabilities of your hardware and can become expensive quickly.

Horizontal scaling, or scaling out, involves adding more servers to handle the incoming load. It's akin to adding more lanes to a highway. This approach is more aligned with cloud-native principles and can often be implemented more cost-effectively. ASP.NET Core applications can benefit significantly from horizontal scaling when deployed in cloud environments, using tools like Kubernetes to manage containerized apps.

An important aspect of both scaling and load balancing is ensuring statelessness in your application. By designing your architecture this way, any server can handle any request, leading to more balanced distributions. ASP.NET Core supports this model well, and leveraging technologies like caching and session management helps maintain state in a distributed way.

When planning the deployment infrastructure for an ASP.NET Core application, consider using tools that make load balancing and automatic scaling straightforward. Cloud services like Azure and AWS provide load balancers and scaling options out of the box, which can be configured to scale based on set metrics automatically. By setting up auto-scaling rules based on CPU usage or request metrics, you ensure that your application adapts dynamically to changes in demand.

Monitoring and analytics play an essential role in scaling and load balancing strategies. Understanding your application's usage patterns helps you make informed decisions about scaling operations. Using tools like Azure Monitor or AWS CloudWatch, you can gather insights into how your application performs under different loads and use this data to adjust your strategies proactively.

Incorporating load balancing and scaling into the design and operation of your ASP.NET Core applications isn't just a technical exercise. It's part of crafting an experience for users that's seamless, reliable, and responsive, even as demand shifts and grows. By mastering these techniques, you're setting the stage for long-term success, allowing your applications to serve more users more effectively.

Ultimately, excellent load balancing and scaling strategies come down to planning, choosing the right tools, and continuously refining your approach based on real-world data. As you continue to build and optimize your ASP.NET Core applications, remember that these techniques are integral to supporting smooth and uninterrupted application performance, helping you not only meet but exceed user expectations.

Conclusion

Here we are, at the culmination of our journey through ASP.NET Core. It's been quite a ride, finding ourselves immersed in the depths of what makes ASP.NET Core such a powerful tool for web development. From setting up your environment to understanding the intricate architecture, you've navigated through the layers that constitute a scalable and robust application framework.

Mastering ASP.NET Core isn't just about knowing the technology; it's about embracing a mindset of continuous learning and adaptation. You're now equipped with the skills to create applications that meet modern demands, tailoring experiences that are as dynamic as they are secure. The web is constantly evolving, and with ASP.NET Core, you're always prepared to stay ahead of the curve.

In your pursuit of excellence, consider the importance of community and collaboration. Engaging with other developers, sharing your experiences, and learning from theirs can enrich your expertise. ASP.NET Core has a vibrant community filled with passionate individuals who are eager to assist and grow alongside you.

Reflecting upon the chapters, remember the foundational concepts like middleware and dependency injection. These elements are the backbone of your applications, ensuring they are not only functional but also flexible and maintainable. As you continue developing, returning to these basics will provide clarity and guidance.

Building your first application was just the start. You've since heightened your understanding of routing, mastered Razor Pages, and grasped the intricacies of MVC architecture. Each step added a new tool to your developer toolkit, empowering you to tackle more complex challenges with confidence.

Your journey wasn't without its challenges— data management with Entity Framework, securing applications, testing, and deployment each came with their own set of hurdles. Yet, overcoming these challenges has reinforced your ability to build applications that are both reliable and scalable.

As you forge ahead, remember that performance optimization is an ongoing process. The strategies for caching, load balancing, and scalability you've learned are crucial for maintaining optimal application performance. Look to the future and envision techniques that will support the growing needs of users.

The landscape of deployment continues to shift, offering a plethora of cloud-based options that promise flexibility and power. You've delved into these possibilities and now have the insight to make informed decisions that best suit your deployment needs.

Your path doesn't end here. It extends further into realms of frontend integration and communication between server and client, where JavaScript frameworks and single-page applications play key roles. Balancing server-side logic with client-side interactivity forms the core of a seamless user experience.

In concluding this chapter of your learning, keep in mind the essence of ASP.NET Core: versatility and efficiency. Your next project is another opportunity to weave together everything you've learned, creating applications that are both innovative and foundationally sound.

Stay curious, stay motivated, and continue building. With the expertise you've gained, there are no limits to what you can achieve. As you apply these lessons to real-world applications, remember that every line of code brings you closer to mastering your craft. Embrace the journey, and celebrate the progress you've made.

Your mastery of ASP.NET Core positions you not only as a developer but as a visionary capable of shaping the future of web applications. The groundwork has been laid, the knowledge acquired, and the scene is set for you to go forth and create something extraordinary. Here's to the incredible possibilities that await!

Appendix A: Tools and Resources for ASP.NET Core Development

Diving into the realm of ASP.NET Core development, you'll find that having the right tools and resources at your disposal can make or break the efficiency and quality of your projects. Let's explore an arsenal of tools that are crucial for any developer aiming to excel in this dynamic ecosystem. From integrated development environments to package managers and beyond, these resources will empower you to wield ASP.NET Core like a seasoned craftsman.

1. Integrated Development Environments (IDEs)

If you're aiming for fluid coding experiences, Visual Studio and Visual Studio Code should be at the top of your list. **Visual Studio**, with its rich set of features, provides powerful debugging and diagnostic tools alongside comprehensive project management capabilities. On the other hand, **Visual Studio Code** is lightweight, versatile, and customizable with a massive library of extensions to tailor your IDE environment to the tee.

2. Command-Line Interfaces (CLIs)

The .NET CLI is indispensable for managing projects, from creating new solutions to tidying up existing ones. It lets you focus on what matters by automating mundane tasks, allowing you to effortlessly compile, publish, and run your applications from the command line. Mastering the .NET CLI commands can significantly streamline your workflow.

3. Package Managers

NuGet stands as the primary package manager for .NET developers, acting as a vast library of reusable code that you can add to your projects with ease. Whether you're in need of essential libraries or want to explore innovative solutions crafted by the community, NuGet provides quick and easy access to a plethora of packages, saving you the time of building everything from scratch.

4. Source Control and Collaboration

Version control systems like Git are pivotal in collaborating across teams and managing code changes efficiently. Platforms such as GitHub or GitLab not only provide seamless collaboration features but also integrate robust tools for issue tracking and continuous integration, essential for modern development practices.

5. Frameworks and Libraries

Incorporating libraries like **ASP.NET Boilerplate** or **ABP Framework** (formerly known as ASP.NET Zero) can give your applications a jump start by offering feature-rich templates and solutions for common scenarios, powerfully aligned with best practices and design patterns in ASP.NET Core development.

6. Documentation and Community

Never underestimate the wealth of information available through Microsoft's official documentation. It's thorough and well-maintained, providing in-depth insights into the internals and best practices of ASP.NET Core. Communities on forums such as Stack Overflow and platforms like Reddit and GitHub Discussions are invaluable for peer support, offering a space to seek guidance and share knowledge.

These tools and resources lay the groundwork for building robust, scalable ASP.NET Core applications, fostering both individual mastery and collaborative success. Treat them as an extension of your development arsenal, and you'll be well-prepared to tackle the challenges and opportunities that come your way in the ever-evolving landscape of web development.